Our Caribbean Civilisation and its Political Prospects

Our Caribbean Civilisation and Its Political Prospects
©2014 Ralph E. Gonsalves

Printed in the United States

This is the first volume in a series entitled
Caribbean Ideas
published by Strategy Forum, Inc.
Kingstown, St. Vincent and the Grenadines

Other titles in the series include
The Case for Caribbean Reparatory Justice

Our Caribbean Civilisation and Its Political Prospects

Three Essays by
Dr. The Honourable Ralph E. Gonsalves
Prime Minister of St. Vincent and the Grenadines

Table of Contents

Foreword

This collection of speeches is the first in the series I call "Caribbean Ideas." The title essay of this collection, "Our Caribbean Civilisation and its Political Prospects," was published in 2009 in the coffee table book entitled *Caribbean Sense of Life*, in which it was the featured essay amidst a collection of quotations from other Caribbean thinkers and hundreds of beautiful black and white photographs. In the introduction of that book I wrote,

> Ideas shape how we think and speak about the world, how we behave, how we see ourselves, individually and in society. Ideas drive imagination; they determine how we conceive the past, the present and the future; they inform our political and social arrangement, our arts and culture, science, technology and religion, our personal relationships and beliefs. Ideas govern what we do and how we do it. Therefore, ideas do matter and the ability to generate them seems increasingly likely to be more important today than raw economic potential, technological advantage, or diplomatic acumen in determining who exercises leadership or creates genuine wealth.

The idea that the Caribbean is a modern civilisation distinct from Western civilisation, or for that matter American civilisation, is as commonly heralded as it is widely disputed. The late Errol Barrow, former Prime Minister of Barbados proposed and Dr. Ralph Gonsalves, the sitting Prime Minister of Saint Vincent and the Grenadines, developed and popularised the notion that we are indeed a civilisation. Jamaican scholar and social critic, the late Rex Nettleford, concurred and saw the island-Caribbean as part of "the geo-cultural area that houses a civilisation with its own inner logic and inner consistency". But Kirk Meighoo, a political scientist from Trinidad, opposes and is of the view that there has not been enough time to form a civilisation; further he insists that a civilisation must provide for its people "a primary point of reference and orientation" and the Caribbean does not, in his view, fit this definition. Meighoo believes, however, that what we do have is a "distinctive Caribbean culture-zone." Edward B. Taylor, the nineteenth century English anthropologist, stated that "Culture is that complex whole which includes knowledge, belief, art, morals, law, custom and any other capabilities acquired by man as a member of society." For Fred Spier, an anthropologist from the University of Amsterdam, culture, using Taylor's definition, equals civilisation. However, the late Leonard Tim Hector, political activist and cricket administrator, challenged the relevance today of the word 'civilisation'; he wondered about its "limited validity" and the need, perhaps, for us to transcend that concept. But he also said: "If civilisation means the greater level of humanity, that is, the greater level of equality, liberty, fraternity and happiness attained by the overwhelming majority of people, then it is a concept, which still has validity. If civilisation means the greater degree of equality between races, between women and men, then it still has validity. If it means the greater harmony between humankind, development and nature, then it still has validity. If civilisation means less centralization of authority and power, and greater distribution of the same, then it still has validity.

This collection of speeches begins with "Our Caribbean Civilisation and its Political Prospects," is followed by "Sovereignty, Independence and Intellectual Thought in the Caribbean: The Legacy of Gordon Lewis" and ends with "Leadership and our Cricketing Culture: Frank Worrell and the Contemporary Caribbean." In the first essay, Dr. Gonsalves establishes his definition of "civilisation" and goes on to illustrate the existence of its elements within the Caribbean; the essays that follow further elaborate on many of those characteristics. Combining scholarship and an easy style of communicating complex ideas, Dr. Gonsalves puts forward what could be considered a robust defense of the idea that the Caribbean is indeed a civilisation.

I. Rhonda King
November 2014

1.
Our Caribbean Civilisation and Its Political Prospects

The Inaugural Lecture in the Distinguished Lecture series Sponsored by CARICOM to Commemorate its Thirtieth Anniversary, held in Post of Spain, Trinidad February 12, 2003.

Preface

I am most pleased to have been asked by CARICOM's Secretary-General, His Excellency Mr. Edwin Carrington, to deliver the inaugural lecture in the Distinguished Lecture Series to mark the thirtieth anniversary of the founding of CARICOM. I take the Secretary-General's invitation as a tribute to St. Vincent and the Grenadines, which has been in the vanguard of regionalism since the 1930s, under a long line of committed regionalists: George Augustus Mc Intosh, Ebenezer Theodore Joshua, Robert Milton Cato and James Fitz-Allen Mitchell. I also take this invitation to address you as a personal honour, a recognition of my many years of unwavering toil in, and for, the regional vineyard. I am the region's newest Prime Minister save and except for the Prime Minister of the Bahamas.

I have been in office for less than two years, and, in that sense I am among the least of the apostles. But I have been in this business for a long, long time. I mark the date of my baptism into politics on October 16, 1968, almost thirty-five years ago, when as a student leader at the University of the West Indies (UWI) in Jamaica I led a massive demonstration into Kingston to protest the then Government's ban on the late Dr. Walter Rodney, a Guyanese national, from returning to his teaching post at the University. We were beaten and tear-gassed by the Jamaican Police and Army. Among the persons in that march and protest whom I led, or misled, that day was a young Trinidad student by the name of Patrick Manning who is now the distinguished Prime Minister of Trinidad and Tobago. I believe that was the first and last time Patrick was beaten and tear-gassed by the security forces of any country. But it was not my last. I wear each of such beatings and tear-gassings as invisible badges of honour in defence and promotion of democracy, peace, justice and regional unity.

I shall point out, not out of vanity or immodesty, but in acknowledgement of my longevity in this regional integration movement, that when sometime in the early 1980s the esteemed Caribbean scholar, the late Dr. Patrick Emmanuel, published his study entitled *Seven Approaches to Regional Integration*, one of the approaches which he analysed was that which is contained in a paper co-authored by Swinburne Lestrade and I in 1971, and later published in *Caribbean Quarterly* in 1972, entitled "The Political Aspects of Integration in the Windward and Leeward Islands". I was then a twenty-five year old graduate student.

So, though I am seemingly the newest boy on the Prime Ministerial block, I have been an old boy on the blocks in Laventille, Trench Town, Paul's Avenue, Colonarie, Roseau, Mona, St. Augustine and Cave Hill.

What Is a Civilisation?

Cuba's revolutionary patriot and national hero, José Marti, wrote aptly and movingly in his celebrated essay of 1891 entitled "Our America" in the following terms:

The prideful villager thinks his hometown contains the whole world; as long as he can stay on as mayor or humiliate the rival who stole his sweetheart or watch his nest egg accumulating in its strong box, he believes the universe to be in good order, unaware of the giants in seven-league boots who can crush him underfoot or the battling comets in the heavens that go through the air devouring the sleeping worlds. Whatever is left in sleepy hometown in our America must awaken. These are not times for going to bed in a sleeping cap, but rather like Juan de Castellano's men, without our weapons for a pillow, weapons of the mind, which vanquish all others. Trenches of ideas are worth more than trenches of stone. A cloud of ideas is a thing no armoured prow can smash through. A vital idea set ablaze before the world at the right moment can, like the mystic banner of the last judgment, stop a fleet of battleships.... We can no longer be a nation of fluttering leaves, spending our lives in the air, our treetop crowned in flowers, humming or creaking by the caprices of sunlight or thrashed and fuelled by tempests. The trees must form ranks to block the seven-leagues giant. It is the hour of reckoning and of marching in unison....

Almost ninety years after José Marti penned those immortal words, the late Prime Minister of Barbados, one of that country's national heroes, Errol Walton Barrow, in a magnificent and incisive speech at the Miami Conference on the Caribbean, November 1986, affirmed, "in the hour of reckoning" the blazing idea of "our Caribbean civilisation" thus:

It is dehumanising and false to view the Caribbean as potential American problems. We are peoples with an identity and a culture and a history – the Parliament of Barbados will be 350 years old in 1989. We don't need lessons in democracy from anyone. However severe the economic difficulties facing the Caribbean, we are viable functioning societies with the intellectual and institutional resources to understand and grapple with our problems. Collectively, we have the resource potential necessary for our continued development and, of course, we have a heritage of exquisite natural beauty entrusted to us. The Caribbean is, after all, a civilisation.

Barrow's affirmation, which I embrace fully, does not meet with universal approval even right here in the Caribbean. Some well-meaning persons, intellectuals among them, side step the idea of "Our Caribbean civilisation" and speak tentatively of a lukewarm notion, "Forward to a Caribbean civilisation" as if it is yet to exist. Some others, cynical about anything authentically Caribbean, parrot the typologies of civilisations established by supposedly authoritative European and American scholars and assert that they find no category called "a Caribbean civilisation". Such persons seek to pigeonhole the Caribbean as being part and parcel of "Western civilisation" without fully appreciating that although "Western civilisation" has contributed significantly to the moulding of "Our Caribbean civilisation", we are so different and distinct as to constitute a civilisation sui generis.

It should be pointed out that many of the typologies of civilisations canvassed in some of the major texts refer to *dominant* civilisations, which have tended to be coterminous with empires, historically. But a civilisation need not possess, nor be in quest of, imperium to be acknowledged as such an entity. Indeed, many discerning writers in this field make that point in one way or another. For example, Felipe Fernandez-Armesto, a long-standing professor of Modern History at Oxford University, in his celebrated volume, *Civilisations,*_identifies a range of civilisations shaped by the sea, including what he calls "small-island civilisations" and "seaboard civilisations".

The concept of "a civilisation" is not easy to define or elucidate. Kenneth Clarke, a witty and astute English observer of civilisations, wrote a book entitled *Civilisation* and he chose not to define "civilisation" but rather "civilised man". He suggests that:

> A civilised man… must feel that he belongs somewhere in space and time; that he consciously looks forward and looks back. And for this purpose it is a great convenience to be able to read and write.

In this sense, therefore, the people of a civilisation must occupy or own their seascape and landscape with a sense of permanence, which goes beyond mere energy and will.

The best exposition on this subject, which I have read, is contained in a fascinating book written by the Mexican Nobel Laureate for Literature, Octavio Paz, under the title *The Labyrinth of Solitude and Other Writings.* Paz had this to say:

> Civilisation is a society's style, its way of living and dying. It embraces the erotic and the culinary arts; dancing and burial; courtesy and curses; work and leisure; rituals and festivals; punishments and rewards; dealings with the dead and with the ghosts who people our dreams; attributes toward women and children, old people and strangers, enemies and allies; eternity and the present; the here and now and the beyond. A civilisation is not only a system of values but a world of forms and codes of behaviour, rules and exceptions. It is society's visible side — institutions, monuments, work, things — but it is especially its submerged, invisible side: beliefs, desires, fears, repressions, dreams.

Of relevance to our discourse this evening is the application by Paz of his notion of "civilisation" in his comparative analysis of Mexico and the United States of America:

> Of course, the differences between Mexico and the United States are not imaginary projections but objective realities. Some are quantitative, and can be explained by the social, economic, and historical development of the two countries. The more permanent ones, though also a result of history, are not easily definable or measurable. I have pointed out that they belong to the realm of civilisation, that fluid zone of imprecise contours in which are fused and confused ideas and beliefs, institutions and technologies, styles and morals fashions and churches, the material culture and the evasive reality which we rather inaccurately call 'the genie des peuples'. The reality to which we give the name civilisation does not allow of easy definition. It is each society's vision of the world and also its feeling about time; there are nations that are hurrying toward the future, and others whose eyes are fixed on the past.

The Evolution of our Caribbean Civilisation

We in this Caribbean — Anglophone, Francophone, Hispanic and Dutch — occupy a particular geographic space which has often been more influential in determining our beings than our history, which admittedly has itself had a profound effect on shaping who we are as individuals, communities, nation-states, and a civilisation. We know that the possibilities contained in both our geography and history jostle, in their manifold connections and contradictions, with their limitations.

Our region's evolution from a culturally plural social arrangement to a relatively integrated Creole society composed almost entirely of migrant peoples from three continents — Africa, Europe and Asia — has made us a unique "small island and seaboard civilisation" within a particular Caribbean seascape and landscape, and with a non-white, creolised majority of peoples. The pre-Columbian heritage, the violence and tutelage of colonialism, the savagery of slavery and the bondage of indentureship involving a population mix of indigenous peoples, Anglo-Saxons, Africans, Portuguese, Indians, Chinese, Jews and Arabs have fashioned a distinctive society. Nowhere else in the world does a society exist like the Caribbean with its particular geographic, historical, sociological and population admixture.

The Caribbean exists as an organic entity in which the whole is more than a summation of the individual parts from the indigenous, Europe, Africa and Asia. The very process, historical and otherwise, of all that coming together in a particular seascape and landscape has made our Caribbean civilisation distinct and distinctive.

Amazingly, although the vast majority of the English-speaking Caribbean peoples are of African descent or possessed of African heritage, there is hardly anyone who insists that this Caribbean is part of an African civilisation. Rather, there is an insistence by many, including presumably informed persons, that this Caribbean is part of the Atlantic or Western civilisation, even though only a small proportion of the population is of Anglo-Saxon, or even European, descent.

This insistence that we are part of Western civilisation stems from a preoccupation with certain visible or formal elements, which have been claimed for that civilisation in our midst, namely:

A classical legacy including the influences of Greek philosophy and rationalism, Roman Law, Latin and Christianity;

Western Christianity itself;
European languages;
The separation of spiritual and temporal authority;
The rule of law;
Social pluralism and civil society;   .
Representative government;
Individualism.

But these values or features of Western civilisation do not manifest themselves to the same extent and in the same form or manner in the Caribbean as they do in Europe or North America, or in other places for that matter. Indeed, the evolved Caribbean society has adopted and adapted these "western" values and elements in such a way as to make both their content and form very Caribbean.

By parallel reasoning, anyone who has seen the exhilarating batting of Vivian Richards or Brian Lara would no doubt realize that the relatively staid English game called cricket has been transformed by Caribbean hands. The rules of the game are identical in England and the Caribbean, but the Caribbean people at cricket, on the field and in the stands, have turned the game into an amazing spectacle with a difference. It goes, too, "beyond a boundary", to use C.L.R. James' telling formulation. In the same way, the imitative Parliaments of the English-speaking Caribbean are but peculiar adaptations of the "Mother of Parliaments" at Westminster, London. Indeed, though similar, Anglo-Caribbean Parliaments are in many ways so different that, at best, they are twisted versions of Westminster.

In any event, as Octavio Paz has reminded us, the civilisation's less visible sides are what have emerged as elusive and peculiar, but which are most defining. Anyone who reads, for example, the novels of George Lamming and V. S. Naipaul, or the poetry of Edward "Kamau" Brathwaite,

17

could hardly be in any doubt about the distinctive creolised nature of our Caribbean civilisation with its African (as emphasized and celebrated by Lamming and Brathwaite) and Indian (as highlighted, and perhaps scorned, by Naipaul) infusions and survivals. Anyone who has read Lloyd Best would know all this even more!

If we are an off-shoot of "western civilisation", or part of it, how is it that our culture, life and living are so obviously different from that of Europe or North America, despite cultural imperialism's bombardment to homogenise us in the image of North America by way of the packaging of a so-called global or universal culture product?

The image that I hold of the Caribbean is that it has emerged, metaphorically, as roughly containing the songs of the Caribs, Arawaks and Amerindians; the rhythm of Africa; the chords of Asia; the melody of Europe; and the homegrown lyrics of the Caribbean itself. These various elements come together as a distinctive, organic whole.

I have identified eight core characteristics that mark out our Caribbean civilisation, namely:

> Geographic, physical and environmental factors of the
> archipelago and seaboard Caribbean;

> A shared history of European conquest, settlement,
> colonialism and empire;

> A population mix derived from indigenous peoples,
> Anglo-Saxons, Portuguese, Africans, Asians,
> Jews and Arabs;

> A core of shared political values both adopted and adapted
> mainly from Western Europe *and* forged through
> the workings of the political process in the Caribbean;

> A distinct cultural matrix fashioned substantially by, and from,
> the cultural milieu of the pre-Columbian Caribbean,
> Africa, Europe and Asia, but with grown evolutions or
> developments;

European languages spoken and written with distinctive
Caribbean nuances, flair and usages;

A productive and technological apparatus, though still
developing and problematic, which sustains the
Caribbean's social, economic and political viability; and

A permanence of being in the Caribbean landscape and
seascape, which goes beyond energy, will and
creative power.

Our Caribbean civilisation is of a small-island and seaboard type. The
islands of the Caribbean, and the countries washed by the Caribbean Sea,
constitute, geographically, the physical base of this civilisation. History,
however, has intervened to cause us at times to speak of our Caribbean
civilisation in a narrower sense, as comprising the chain of islands from
the Bahamas to Trinidad and Tobago and the countries on mainland
South America, Belize and Guyana, which have shared a common British
colonization. Politics and economic necessity have pushed the idea of
"our Caribbean civilisation" to embrace Surinam (a former Dutch colony
on the South American mainland) and Haiti (a former colony of France
and the first independent black nation-state in the Western Hemisphere),
both of which are members of the Caribbean Community (CARICOM).
Still, the evolving political and economic necessity and desirability will,
in time, lead us all to build on the existing geographic and historical
bases, and so prompt us to embrace a wider notion of "our Caribbean
civilisation" to include the island-states of Cuba, the Dominican Republic,
Puerto Rico, the U.S. Virgin Islands, the Dutch and French Antilles, and
all the other Central and South American countries that are washed by
the Caribbean Sea.

Our Caribbean civilisation can be easily contrasted with what has been
termed "the American civilisation". To be sure, just as in the Caribbean,
the American civilisation is peopled largely by descendants of migrants
(voluntary and forced) plus a smattering of indigenous persons. But,
in the United States of America, the population is overwhelmingly
Caucasian; in the Caribbean, it is, by far, a creolised, non-white majority.
In the Caribbean there is a process of creolisation; in America there are
the contradictory pulls of assimilation into a dominant white culture or

separation. The Caribbean civilisation is of a "small island and seaboard" type; the American civilisation is substantially continental. America's civilisation has emerged as a dominant global force, with neo-imperial manifestations; the Caribbean civilisation lies in the hinterland of that neo-empire, daily and profoundly influenced by it.

Still, America's presence in the Caribbean's daily living and production does not diminish our civilisation's unique or distinctive formation in a particular time and geographic space, as a producing society, not a parasitic one, with an inter-connected and sophisticated social, cultural and political umbrella.

The Caribbean, with a long and noble pre-Columbian history, was forcibly pushed by Europeans into the vortex of mercantile capitalism, then industrial capitalism and later monopoly capitalism, and shoved away from a path of autochthonous development. The social formations, which evolved in the political economy in the Caribbean, have been inextricably linked to the requisites of these external relations of exchange. These networks of production relations and exchange relations, which have underdeveloped the region, have, at the same time, provided a productive base pregnant with possibilities, despite inherent contradictions and limitations, for the sustenance of our Caribbean civilisation. Indeed, the Caribbean's political economy, both in its historical evolution and contemporary manifestations, has substantially fashioned our very civilisation.

Our Caribbean civilisation has been very much shaped by the sea. The evidence of this in our region abounds from time immemorial: the peopling of our Caribbean; its trading; its economy and commerce, ancient and modern; its daily living and eating; its culture and its thinking. All these facets of life and production have been moulded, even determined, by the sea. The evocative poetry of our region's premier literary titan, Derek Walcott, draws its meaning, thought, ideas and imagery substantially from the sea.

The overwhelming presence of the sea in "small island and seaboard civilisations" has been highlighted by Fernandez–Armesto:

The sea can shape island civilisations either by confining them or linking them to other islands. Either way, proximity to the sea is such a powerful feature of any environment which includes it that it dwarfs all the others. Whatever the nature of the soil or temperature, the relief or biota, if the sea is at hand it has a shaping force. Nearness to the shore moulds one's outlook and affects the way one thinks. The sea is awesome because it is intractable, untrappable; it changes everything it touches without being easily changed in turn.... It reshapes shorelines, erodes coasts, gulps swards and cities, and hews continents. At us land-creatures it flings weather systems which, after all our millennia of civilisation, symbolise the continuing feebleness of our power over the environment. The sea has no appointed limits, except in the pious cravings of the prayerful. It is a part of the chaos that survived creation. It makes us feel small.

Strangely, our Caribbean civilisation has yet to reflect in public policy the real value and significance of the sea that joins us all. To be sure, each country in the region has its own Ministry of Fisheries, but each such ministry functions like an island unto itself, with very little cooperative, much less integration of, effort. We still cannot yet fix properly "the problem" — if that is what it is — of Barbadian fishermen who go in search of flying fish off Tobago, or of all types of Caribbean fisherfolk trawling off the fishing grounds in St. Vincent and the Grenadines. There is still, too, no maritime delimitation agreement between contiguous Caribbean nation-states. Frankly, our Caribbean civilisation has done very little to exploit or command the resources of our seas. It is true that we do a little fishing, and our lovely beaches draw tourists whom we rightly seek and welcome. But do we, for example, know what truly lies under the waters of our seas? Is there oil in commercially viable quantities beneath our seabed from Trinidad going north through Grenada, St. Vincent and the Grenadines and St. Lucia, and east to Barbados? Are we working on this issue jointly or separately? These and many other such vital public policy queries can be justifiably posed for practical answering!

Historically, small islands have been among the poorest places in the world. The great historian Fernand Braudel derisively labelled most of the islands of the Mediterranean in the sixteenth century as "hungry worlds" or "prisons of a precarious life". It is a perspective that finds resonance in the Naipaulian gloom of our Caribbean's alleged lack of creativity and its presumed nothingness.

But we know, too, that many small islands, historically, have triumphed over their smallness and their "islandness", for example, Malta and Venice. In the modern era we can point to Taiwan, Singapore, Hong Kong, and, to a large extent, even our own Barbados. Is our Caribbean civilisation in the twenty-first century to succumb a gloomy Naipaulian future, become a prison of precarious living and bottom out as a wreck of a potential paradise? Or is it going to be on a path of further evolvement, advancement and development?

These are critical questions in this challenging epoch of an increasingly globalised world in which there is undoubtedly a quest by certain powerful forces in the North Atlantic to impose a "new world order". Legitimate questions thus arise for our civilisation: "What's new?" "Which world"? and "Why doesn't our Caribbean civilisation combine, in political and economic terms, to meet more efficaciously the challenges of the new, globalised, world order?"

The future of our Caribbean civilisation hinges, in large measure, on our provision of relevant and practical answers to the host of queries, among others, which I have been posing. The answers revolve around us acting together in solidarity, within our respective nations and across the region, in the interest of our own humanisation and the further ennoblement of our Caribbean civilisation. I say all this not for political effect, but with a solemnity and a profound seriousness, informed by a careful comparative study over many years, fashioned on the anvil of experience and forged in the cauldron of political struggle.

A civilisation, and its prospects, is not to be assessed merely on the basis of the outstanding achievements of individuals within it. But clearly an abundance of individual excellence in various fields of human endeavour is an indicator of the progress of a civilisation. In the Caribbean such individual excellence is extensive. We know the outstanding examples; there is thus no need to recite them here.

However, the true measure of our Caribbean civilisation is not in the individual efforts of these distinguished persons, but in the community and solidarity of the people, as a whole, in the process of nation building:

the ordinary workers in agriculture, industry, fisheries and tourism;

the professionalism and extra efforts of health personnel, educators, police officers and social workers;

the collective spirit and endeavours of the youths in tackling community problems;

the day-to-day travails of women in keeping their families together and guiding their off-spring;

the struggles of the poor in addressing their housing needs, with or without state assistance;

the daily grind of ordinary folk in their quest for greater democratic controls on the state administration, and for justice;

the splendid dominance of the West Indies Cricket team, and the Cuban baseball squad, in their respective sports internationally for nearly two decades;

the fifty-odd years of tertiary education provided so far by the University of the West Indies, and the over two hundred and seventy years of similar work by the University of Havana;

the heroic battles of the Cuban people in defence and promotion of their sovereignty, national independence and internationalism;

the striving of our sportsmen, sportswomen, cultural creators and writers of the creative imagination, professionals of all kinds, peasants and workers of excellence;

the building of friendships internationally between peoples and nations; and generally the collective actions of our peoples in the arts, culture, production, architecture, religion, journalism, politics and sports.

All these endeavours, and more, of the civilised whole ennoble us. Contrary actions diminish our civilisation.

The Integrative Efforts of our Caribbean Civilisation

Each civilisation possesses several apparatuses, including those lodged in the political and economic spheres. Indeed, the praxis — theory and practice — which manifests itself in a civilisation, combines the social individual, the community, the nation and the nation-state. The Caribbean, being a regional category with geographical, historical, social, cultural, economic and political dimensions, necessarily articulates the on-going quest for socio-economic and political integration regionally. All these are factors extant in our civilisation. The big query is: What is to be the nature of the institutionalised political expression of our Caribbean civilisation?

Currently, (in the year 2003) there are three concentric circles of integration in the Caribbean, each with points of contact and relevance to the others. The outermost concentric circle is the Association of Caribbean States (ACS), which consists of all countries washed by the Caribbean Sea; a Greater Caribbean so to speak, namely: the fourteen members of the Caribbean Community (CARICOM), the Spanish-speaking countries of Colombia, Costa Rica, Cuba, Dominican Republic, El Salvador, Guatemala, Honduras, Mexico, Nicaragua, Panama, Venezuela; and associate members from the French and Dutch Antilles. The ACS addresses four issues mainly: trade, tourism, transportation and technology.

The second concentric ring is the Caribbean Community (CARICOM) with its wide-ranging mechanisms for functional cooperation, its coordinated arrangements, more less, as a free trade area and customs union, and its aim to build a Caribbean Single Market and Economy (CSME).

The third, innermost concentric circle of regional integration is the Organisation of Eastern Caribbean States (OECS) with membership, full and associate, of the six independent states, and the former British dependent territories of Anguilla, British Virgin Islands and Montserrat. The Treaty of Basseterre, which established the OECS in 1981, lists eighteen areas of functional cooperation within a political-administrative superstructure which is proximately confederal. It is evident, though, that useful as these three concentric circles of integration are, they do not measure up to the challenges at hand for our civilisation. There are factors which overwhelmingly predispose and induce us to deeper union. Yet we are stalled. Devising more advanced models of regional integration is not the problem, since creative thinkers abound in our Caribbean civilisation to do so. The real issues are contained in the following three queries:

What is the most advanced model of regional integration that the political market nationally can bear?

Do the leaders of the region — political, economic, community and social — and the people themselves possess the political will and readiness to go beyond the parameters of the individual nation-states and embrace a union deeper than that which currently exists?

What is to be done right now to construct, or prepare for the construction of, a deeper union between CARICOM countries, or at least between those who are ready and determined to go forward?

Let us attempt to answer these and other ancillary questions. There is currently a paradox which grips the individual nation states of our region in the context of a deteriorating international economic situation which the British Chancellor of the Exchequer, Gordon Brown, has correctly depicted as the worst in thirty years. The paradox is this: the awful condition of the international political economy prompts the political leaders and other elites in the region to look outwards from the bastions of their fragile nation-states in search of a deeper, though ill-defined and even inchoate, regionalism *but*, at the same time, the ever-growing and compelling domestic demands or requisites in the respective nation-states so pre-occupy these same leaders or elites that the regional becomes tangential, or even marginal, to their day-to-day work. Indeed, some may say, and not without some justification, that the sheer weight of the national travails immobolises, or even paralyses, the national leaders to such an extent that the regional departs from the core of their consciousness in their day-to-day decision-making. It is in this context that the initiative, nay, the clarion call, of the Prime Minister of the Republic of Trinidad and Tobago, my dear friend Patrick Manning, to cause the leaders of CARICOM to assemble here in Port-of-Spain to address the twin issues of governance and deeper union in the region, is of immeasurable significance. I applaud him for being a stalwart of regionalism. This is not a new persona for him. This was his commitment since first I knew him, when we were both students at the University of the West Indies in Jamaica. Over the years, that commitment has evolved into an article of faith for the further ennoblement of our Caribbean civilisation.

Every single Head of Government in the Caribbean is a committed regionalist, though, too often, some of us can so easily be imprisoned by ghosts of the past or constrained by electoral imperatives arising from a narrow territorial nationalism, or simply held back by a fear of the future without the institutional props of the individual nation-state, a category which is becoming increasingly anachronistic, save in a narrow juridical sense.

The Martiniquan intellectual, Edouard Glissant, in his fascinating book, *Caribbean Discourse: Selected Essays*, issues an admonishment to us, which I believe we ought to heed:

> As soon as we see a political program, no matter how radical, hesitate in the face of choosing a Caribbean identity, we can offer the certain diagnosis of a hidden desire to be restrained by the limits imposed by non-history, by a more or less shameful alignment with (metropolitan) values that one can never, and with good reason, manage to control, by a fatal inability to have a sense of one's destiny.

This Caribbean identity demands an institutional political expression of the deepest kind possible for it not to languish in inchoateness, and perhaps eventually wither and die. This is a great cause, and great causes are not won by doubtful men and women.

I acknowledge, as a practical man of affairs, that although the challenges in our region's political economy and society cannot be properly met without a maximalist approach to deeper union, the minds of men and women in the region are so fettered by considerations unconnected to this central reality, not a dream, that they will not at this time entertain maximalism in this regard. Still, the creeping minimalism, which afflicts the regional integration movement currently, will condemn us to a further thirty years of increasing irrelevance and worse. We act as though we do not see before our very eyes that some countries in the region are hurtling swiftly toward a condition of failed societies. It is true that an incidence of being a state is that it has the legitimate monopoly on physical coercion, yet in a growing number of Caribbean countries the dons, the gangs, organised and non-organised criminals, challenge this monopoly. In the process, ordinary right-thinking persons begin to question the very legitimacy and relevance of the state itself. What is the purpose of a nation-state if it cannot guarantee its citizens and visitors, in practice, a condition which protects their security and personal safety? That is a query which is increasingly posed in this region. And I am not an alarmist.

So, when individual nation-states find it increasingly difficult, or even find themselves unable, to address efficaciously the central concerns of people, they inevitably concentrate on sideshows. But the main event is where the action ought to be. The central questions can only be dealt with in a deeper union and reconstructed democratic governance.

I suggest that, between the maximalist quest and the minimalist incoherence in regionalism, there is a large area for urgent activism. I advocate a sturdy, confederal political arrangement, which, for short hand, I label *European Union Plus*. That is to say, to move swiftly to an integrated whole similar, though not identical, to that of the European Union, *plus* other home-grown variations, additions or evolutions.

I do admit that, for a variety of practical reasons, some Caribbean countries may not at first be able to join in this deeper regional venture. But I feel sure that all, or some, of the countries of the eastern and southern Caribbean may find this a practical fit. In such a confederal union, the centre does what can better be done there, but in communion with the unit territories, and the individual nation-states focus mainly on those matters which give a better life and sustenance nationally to their communities and peoples. The details in such a confederal arrangement are not difficult to work out. But in whatever we do, the people must be fully and meaningfully involved, from start to finish.

To me, it makes little sense for us to proceed in fits and starts in the regional integration movement and dump into the CARICOM and the OECS Secretariats a host of additional functional cooperation tasks, without the means or the political superstructure to match. Integration has never been, and will never be, a series of technical functions. It is a profoundly political exercise. It is escapism and irresponsibility not to so acknowledge this *in practice*. It is, basically, for this reason that the CSME and other regional initiatives or mechanisms are faltering. But it does not have to be like this; we must correct all this and build immediately upon it. Despite the limitations, our condition is pregnant with possibilities.

Historically, one of the central problems of regional integration efforts in the Caribbean has been their tendency to integrate state systems, not peoples or the civilisation. The West Indies federation emphasised the establishment of formal governmental institutions which were isolated from the people; CARICOM has focused on trading arrangements and the efficacy of the Secretariat; and the OECS has, as its raison d'etre, eighteen areas of functional cooperation. All of these have been important and, at the second remove, touch and connect with the people, but in none of these unity frameworks has the issue of the freedom of movement of peoples been favourably addressed, or the travel of Caribbean people from one regional country to another been made hassle-free, except recently in the OECS for OECS nationals.

Indeed, while the technology and availability of regional transport, air and sea, have made it easier for intra-Caribbean travel, the contemporary states have put immigration barriers in place which have made it more difficult than in colonial times for nationals of one Caribbean country to enter another. It even goes further than this: Guyanese visitors are, by and large, looked upon with grave suspicion by the immigration authorities of sister CARICOM countries; Americans and Canadians are welcomed with open arms in Barbados, whilst St. Lucians and Vincentians are generally treated as unwanted strangers at the gates; Rastafarians are instinctively discriminated against by the immigration and customs officers in practically every country in the region, possibly save and except for Jamaica; and Barbadians are caricatured as "smart men" who must be watched closely at ports of entry and beyond. All this is totally unacceptable.

No federation or confederation or some lesser form of union can truly survive these indignities and irrationalities. To be sure, CARICOM governments have sought to lessen these hardships in the case of graduates of Caribbean universities and other selected categories of professionals. But, useful as this is, it has regrettably strengthened the impression in the minds of ordinary Caribbean folk that 'this integration business' is for the elite. Unless and until a thorough pro-active programme of encouraging intra-Caribbean travel and residence is devised by Caribbean governments, regional integration or political union would not command the requisite degree of popular support as it should. To their credit, last year, the OECS countries relaxed some of the barriers to freedom of movement of their peoples.

The fears and prejudices which drive the immigration policies of many Caribbean states in relation to each other's citizens are without foundation. The notion that criminals would cross borders undetected, ignores the huge potential in coordinating police activities and denies the fact that each Caribbean country has its own ballooning body of homegrown criminals. Roughly, in this regard, the practical effect of more open borders for each other's nationals in the region would be an equalization of travel by criminals. The same principle applies to the migration of unemployed persons. Indeed, easier migration of the unemployed in the region is likely to result in more employment since the tendency of migrants is to take any honest work in their adopted lands which they would not have taken in the land of their birth. Migration and initiative go hand in hand: that is the lesson of human civilisation the world over.

Two options face our Caribbean civilisation:

The well-beaten path of the post-independence period which is likely to lead to adsorption by the metropolitan centres, loss of independence, cultural domination, continued underdevelopment and, in all probability, increasing misery for our people; and the creative alternative of the Caribbean as an independent, authentic civilisation, which blossoms and bears fruits abundantly within a political union of the region.

If the first option is pursued, I predict that within fifty years the Caribbean could be working out an associate status with the United States of America or Europe. We would be offered some variant of the Platt Amendment of early twentieth century Cuba or some benign, or not so benign, twist to the current Puerto Rican model. If we remain independent, it would be in name only.

Chatoyer, Toussaint L'Overture, Grantley Adams, the Manleys, Errol Barrow, Eric Williams, Maurice Bishop, Cheddi Jagan, Forbes Burnham, Robert Bradshaw, Milton Cato and thousands upon thousands of our patriotic forebears would have lived, worked and died in vain. Imagine the possible, even probable, scenario if we do not take appropriate stock and alter course: within fifty years we would be voting in a referendum to determine our status in relation to the United States of America or Europe.

Do not for one moment believe that I am dwelling in the realm of fantasy. Already in the United States of America, scholars and policy-makers, both liberal and conservative, are raising the imminent query: are the countries of the Caribbean viable political and social entities in the new millennium?

The arrogance of this question can only be answered decisively, by us, if we pursue the second option, which is grounded in the recognition of ourselves as a civilisation.

It is inescapable that, in this new millennium, the Caribbean will be integrated as one. The relevant questions, however, are: who or what will direct the integration, and on whose terms will the integration be consummated?

It is either we, the Caribbean people, take control of the integration process in the interest of our own humanisation, or regional integration will be driven and effected by others, in their own interests. We must therefore keep our eyes on the ball and not swipe outside the off-stump.

The second option demands a package of policies, many of which have been detailed in official reports, some party manifestoes, academic publications and by the West Indian Commission headed by 'Sonny' Ramphal. It requires a population which is educated, skilled, and conscious in its Caribbean-ness, and which becomes imbued with new and more productive attitudes to work; a population which works hard and in a disciplined manner; and a population which avoids laziness, criminality and vagabondry. It calls, too, for high quality leadership of our Caribbean civilisation, which eschews the debilitating political disease of a learned helplessness and studied pessimism.

Let us shake off the bleak past of yesterday and become optimistic for tomorrow, which Martin Carter of Guyana so beautifully and poetically mapped out for us in 1954:

I come from the nigger yard of yesterday
Leaping from the oppressor's hate and the scorn of myself.
I come to the world with scars upon my soul
Wounds on my body, fury in my hands.
I turn to the histories of men and the lives of the peoples.
I examine the shower of sparks and the wealth of the dreams.
I am pleased with the glories and sad with the sorrows,
rich with the riches, poor with the loss.
From the nigger yard of yesterday, I come with my burden.
To the world of tomorrow I turn with my strength.

This anthem for our civilisation, this pledge for our future, should inspire us, and draw out of us that which is good and noble. In the process, let us avoid the condition in which the best of us lack all conviction and the worst set the pace with the passionate intensity of territorial chauvinists.

2.

Sovereignty, Independence and Intellectual Thought in the Caribbean: The Legacy of Gordon R. Lewis

Address Delivered at the Gordon Lewis Symposium, University of the West Indies, Mona, Jamaica on October 01, 2010

Today, our Caribbean is engaged in a profound search for a way out of its enveloping socio-economic and political challenges of a magnitude not experienced since independence. This symposium on the intellectual work of Gordon R. Lewis and its impact on political thought in our region is bound to assist. This Welshman's encounter with our Caribbean has produced intellectual insights and political analysis of both context and text which have shone with a brightness which illuminates and not blinds. He has caused us to reflect on overarching themes, grounded in an admixture of geography, culture, political sociology, the literature of the creative imagination, political economy and political praxis, with a freshness and creativity which are now more needed them ever.

All this jumps out at us as Gordon Lewis traverses the growth of the modern West Indies, the intellectual and ideational foundations of our Caribbean, the independence of Puerto Rico and our Caribbean, the despoiling of the jewel that was revolutionary Grenada, the integration and political sociology of our multi-languaged region.

Like the Barbadian and Caribbean poet, H. A. Vaughn in his minor classic "Revelation", Gordon Lewis saw the Caribbean and its people as manifestations of a beauty which escaped colonial schools. As such Lewis railed against those who caused us to "keep tight lips for burnished beauty nearer home" and who urged us to prate, to extol, as ideal that which came from Greece, Rome, and "the face that launched a thousand ships". This elemental and uplifting embrace by Lewis of the intrinsic magnificence of our people stands in contrast to some who have come from the metaphoric "niggeryard of yesterday" with the scorn of themselves arising, seemingly paradoxically, from the oppressor's hate. Like Martin Carter of Guyana, Lewis saw the consciousness of our being as our central strength for our challenging tomorrows. To be sure, Gordon Lewis acknowledged and explored sharply our region's limitations and weaknesses but he always returned to our strengths and possibilities. Truth is beauty, too. This dialectical thought process never allowed him to descend into a trendy learned helplessness of prelates, political poseurs, and the pontiffs of a manufactured consensus emanating from international financial institutions. Lewis was always positive, upbeat, and optimistic about our region's possibilities.

Recently, I was reading some essays authored by the Franco-Czech novelist, Milan Kundera, and published in 2009 under the title, *Encounter*. It struck me that he was onto a Lewis theme while he was discussing Aimé Cesaire, Patrick Chamoiseau, and Martinique. Kundera was seeking to locate a margin, which every people searches for, between its own home and the world. This margin or realm between national and global contexts, Kundera calls "the median context". For example, a Chilean has Latin America as its median context; a Swede has its Scandanavian bloc. But some countries such as Austria, Greece, and Turkey have a difficulty identifying its median context. Kundera advises that:

There are some nations whose identity is characterized by duality, by the complexity of their median context, and that's precisely what gives them their particularity.

As to Martinique, I would say the same thing: the coexistence of various different median contexts there is what makes for the particularity of its culture. Martinique: a multiple intersection; a crosswords among the continents; a tiny slip of land where France, Africa, the Americas meet.

Yes, that's beautiful. Very beautiful, except that France, Africa, America don't care much. In today's world that voice of small entities is barely heard.

Martinique: the encounter of a great cultural complexity with a great solitude.

Incidentally, for those who contests this lack of caring or hearing by the metropolises for, and of, the Caribbean may learn otherwise if they consult the biography of Bill Clinton entitled *My Life* (2004) and that of Tony Blair, *A Journey* (2010). These two western leaders of "the third way" mentioned the Caribbean only fleetingly. In neither biography did the mention warrant inclusion in the comprehensive index. The Caribbean was simply ignored.

Gordon Lewis was partly consumed in seeking to understand the "great cultural complexity" called the Caribbean, its impact on our region's society, economy and polity, and its median context or destiny in a united or integrated Caribbean amidst the solitude of island nationalisms or even chauvinisms. How to bring together, optimally in a coherent unit, the Caribbean islands and territories each awash with it peculiarities but all conjoined by overwhelming commonalities, remains an enduring problematic.

Gordon Lewis accepted almost entirely the analysis and prescription for an integrated Caribbean of his friend, Dr. Eric Williams, the legendary historian and political leader from Trinidad and Tobago. Lewis saw the collapse of the West Indian federal venture of the early 1960s not so much as the consequence of bickering political personalities or disruptive island nationalisms but as fundamentally a failure of conception. For him, the weak apparatus, constitutionally, of the central government in the Federation was a colonial construct derived from a classical notion of a federation but which in the Caribbean amounted to an unworkable confederation. His preference was for a much stronger central government as envisaged in Williams' *Economics of Nationhood*. It is to be seriously doubted, however, that such a model would have survived the political market-place. It would be a simplistic error to conclude, as Lewis did not, that a "secessionist" Jamaica was or is the only bull in the regional china shop. In the early 1990s, Sir James Mitchell, Prime Minister of St. Vincent and the Grenadines, found out that his advocacy of a "unitary state" or at least a "strong federal centre" for a Windwards-Leewards Political Union was shot down as pie-in-the-sky dreaming.

We are all still absorbed with this issue of regional governance in an integrated Caribbean. The Grand Anse Declaration of 1989, the Revised Treaty of Chaguaramas of 2001, the Rose Hall Declaration of 2003, the Gonsalves-led Prime Ministerial Working Group of 2003 to 2007, the Vaughn Lewis Technical Working Group of 2007, and the recent Montego Bay Decision of 2010 are all staging posts in the journey to resolve the intractable governance conundrum in the Caribbean Community (CARICOM). The Economic Union Treaty of the Organisation of Eastern Caribbean States (OECS) of 2010 takes the practical pursuit of a governance solution along the continuum away from confederalism but not yet to a full federal exercise. The jury is still out on its efficacy, although its future is promising.

Interestingly, Gordon Lewis's starting point for his penetrating analysis of the Caribbean begins with his profound appreciation of nature's impact. It is an obvious fact but so easily missed by some other accomplished commentators. The first sentence in his magisterial analysis published in 1968 and known to us as *The Growth of the Modern West Indies*, is quite arresting:

> The most striking single feature of the Caribbean chains of the West Indies society is, perhaps, their unique geographical position.

It is almost akin to the first line, too, in Roy Strong's 1966 volume, *History of Britain*: "Britain is an island and that fact is more important than any other in understanding its history."

This "most striking single feature" of the Caribbean's "unique geographical position" encompasses its location, the spread of the archipelago, its geology, its landscape and seascape, and its climate. But for Lewis, nature is the starting point, not the end point. So, he tells us:

The real oppressions of West Indian life, however, have not been so much those of nature and geography as those of history and culture. If the region has been since slavery Emancipation (1834) nothing much more than a geographical expression, that had been due in the main part, to the legacy of its colonial history in all of its manifold forms. It is nurture , not nature, that has produced from the historical beginnings, that Balkanisation of the regional government and politics. The real barriers have been the artificial ones, linguistic, monetary, commercial, for the mutual ignorance and sometimes mutual hostilities of the various island populations, even when they are all English-speaking, stem from the fact that colonisation decreed that the avenues of communication should be between each individual West Indian fief and London, rather than between the territories themselves.

...Political imperialism, in brief, explains more than any other single factor, the present disunity of the region, the aimlessness so distressingly apparent since the collapse of the federal venture in 1962, with the resultant trend towards micro-nationalism. Cultural imperialism, in its turn, by seeking through education to convert the West Indian person into a coloured English gentleman produced the contemporary spectacle of the West Indian as a culturally disinherited individual, an Anglicised colonial set with an Afro-Asian cultural environment, caught between the dying Anglophile world and the new world of Caribbean democracy and nationalism seeking to be born.

This bundle of crisscrossing issues, their historical and sociological underpinnings, their political expressions, and the people's quest for sovereignty, democracy, and an enhanced condition of living, are what preoccupied Gordon Lewis on his extended and productive Caribbean sojourn. As he had put it himself, his prolonged residence in the Caribbean area, along with his strategically-located perch in Puerto Rico, had given him "the right to be heard". And we are hearing him clearly.

Lewis had a scientist's instinctive aversion to facile, simplistic, and over-stretched formalistic explanations to the real condition of the Caribbean. To be sure, he was curious and intellectually adventurous but he never allowed his curiosity and adventurousness to take him to fanciful flights from what was closest and most concrete. Much of the celebrated writings by too many intellectuals in our region and elsewhere stray too easily from scientific observation and analysis of the actual condition of life in society. On this we can all learn from Lewis.

Indeed, this subject is an enduring one in intellectual thought. In a remarkable book entitled *The Conscience of Words and Earwitness*, published in 1987, the distinguished European Nobel Laureate for Literature, Elias Canetti, had this say:

> Among the most sinister phenomena in intellectual history is the avoidance of the concrete. People have had a conscious tendency to go first after the most remote things, ignoring everything they stumble over close by. The élan of outgoing gestures, the boldness and adventure of expeditions to faraway places camouflage their motives. The not infrequent goal is to avoid what lies near because we are not up to it.... But the situation of mankind today, as we all know, is so serious that we have to turn to what is closest and most concrete.

Much of political science literature in the Caribbean, before and after Gordon Lewis, has been pre-occupied with legal-institutional analysis, the poring over of survey data of this or that opinion poll, impressionistic behavioural studies, the political sparring between competing elites, and over-playing the importance to political understanding of "charisma" or "hero-crowd" conceptions. It is not that these do not form part of the analytic mix which leads towards a comprehensive theory of explanation, but as stand-alone offerings they become momentary, ahistorical snap-shots rather than a thorough-going explanation.

Let us illustrate all this with Lewis' robust rebuke of Archibald W. Singham, the well-known Sinhalese political scientist who lived and toiled lovingly among us for many years, on the issue of charismatic leadership as an explanatory frame for Caribbean politics. Singham was to elaborate his thesis in his celebrated volume entitled *The Hero and the Crowd in a Colonial Polity* and published by Yale University Press in 1967. Lewis is unlikely to have read Singham's book before his *Growth of the Modern West Indies* went to press, but he had certainly read the Singham thesis in the latter's mimeographed paper entitled *Political Crisis and Electoral Change in a Colonial Society* which was presented at the 1963 annual meeting of the American Political Science Association.

In referencing Singham's 1963 paper, Lewis joined the battle in the following terms:

> The cause célèbre of the battle in the Windwards was, of course, the phenomenal rise of Gairy and Gairyism after 1950. A West Indian political scientist (meaning Singham) has attempted to see the movement in Weberian terms. But it is doubtful if a schematic analysis that sees Gairy as the Weberian charismatic leader and the Grenada Government as the embodiment of rationalistic bureaucracy does anything more than describe the institutional superstructure while ignoring, except for a brief description, the social class struggle out of which Gairyism emerged; not to mention the fact that the procedure attributes motivational factors to the actors of the drama and seriously distorts the meaning of what actually happened. For "charisma" is not a self-generating first cause; it grows out of deep social crisis. Gairy's providential return to Grenada in 1946 from the Aruba oil fields — the nursery of West Indian agitational leadership — did not create the crisis. It merely provided the crisis with its appropriate leadership. To be properly understood, it must be seen in terms of (1) its socio-cultural environment and (2) the old-style Grenadian political leadership that preceded it.

This is compelling and persuasive stuff. But it is clear that Lewis is not Marxian in that he subscribes simply to "social classes" as the sole explanatory fulcrum or that "social class struggle", simpliciter, is the motor force of history. It is true that Lewis searches for explanations embedded in

39

the social and historical condition which gave rise to Gairy and Gairyism but that involves a host of factors, a veritable parallelogram of forces, including class, race, culture, colonialism, the crisis of underdevelopment, the people's aspirations, class struggles, and the peculiarities of particular leaderships. These Lewis combines into a whole which he observes in their dialectical inter-connections over historical time.

In the process, Lewis contributes to our creative, unfettered thinking, but linked always to our real condition and our quest for a better life as a sovereign people. I thus recommend to all a re-read of Lewis' final chapter in *The Growth of the Modern West Indies* entitled "The Challenge of Independence" and his *Notes on the Puerto Rican Revolution*, published in 1974.

Gordon Lewis was absolutely sure that "independence means a national stock-taking of heroic proportions". No institution is to be spared review, renewal, appropriate alteration or re-creation. The political party, the trade union, the church, and the formal institutions of government were, in his view, to be subject to overhaul, restructuring, enhancement. This correct prescription is still an urgent prognosis at hand; at best, it is still a work-in-progress with a long way to go.

Moreover, Lewis is compelling in what he considers among the central challenges of independence. He rightly opines:

> It is not enough, with independence, to be merely against something, however justifiably. One must be for something. The social energies of newly liberated peoples, hitherto underutilised in the colonial system, now await the invention of new institutions and new purposes to fulfill themselves. The West Indies, after some early false starts, are thus clearly on the move. The basic questions of their future revolve not around the movement itself, but around the direction in which it will propel itself.

Independence, for Lewis, means, too, "a new positive citizenship". According to him:

A new type of public opinion must be organised as the popular base of that citizenship. Equally, a new sense of personal responsibility, of personal involvement, must grow up, for much of what passes for new national spirit is frequently a sterile anti-colonial prejudice.

This call for personal responsibility and collective ownership of the society and political process resonates with all of us who champion enhanced good governance in this part of our Earthly City. This "personal responsibility" and "collective ownership" are vital cornerstones for the further ennoblement of our Caribbean civilisation and its institutional, political expressions.

In the case of Puerto Rico, Lewis was passionate about Puerto Rico becoming an independent, socialist, and democratic republic. In his *Notes on the Puerto Rican Revolutions*, he thundered, as a public and activist intellectual:

> The final argument for independence...is that it will finally release the hitherto suppressed moral and spiritual energies of the Puerto Rican people in the service of a new society based on the maxim of equality. These energies have hitherto been curtailed and limited by authoritarian and elitist structures of government.... Only a thorough destruction of that system can make way for popular, day-to-day political participation and industrial and agricultural self-government on the part of the workers. Only then can the remarkable moral and social qualities of the Puerto Rican people...receive their full expression.

Given Lewis' anti-colonial, anti-imperialist, socialist-oriented, and regionalist stance, it was painful for him and all those of like mind to experience, even at a distance, the heartache and sorrow of the collapse of the Grenada Revolution in October 1983 and the almost concurrent invasion by the United States of America. His rendering of this sad period of our history and politics is worth re-reading, too. The consequences still reverberate.

In my forthcoming autobiographical volume entitled *The Making of "The Comrade": The Political Journey of Ralph Gonsalves*, (forthcoming October 2010) I have written on this subject, in part, as follows:

> The death of the Grenada Revolution opened up the way for the triumph of reactionary and backward forces in the Caribbean under the imperial hegemony of Ronald Reagan's USA and Margaret Thatcher's Britain. Creative intellectual thought in the region was stifled as the Washington consensus fashioned by the International Monetary Fund (IMF) and the World Bank took root in our universities, regional institutions, major political parties, the mass media, and the churches. The collapse of centrally-planned regimes in the Soviet Union and Eastern Europe consolidated the sense of American triumphalism as the multi-polar, or even bipolar, world gave way to a unipolar American ascendancy. In the region, many comrades on "the left" grew weary, disillusioned and demoralised. Only those with a correct perspective of the contradictory evolution of historical forces, a realistic assessment of the possibilities and limitations of our condition, and an unswerving commitment to change, whatever the personal costs, were prepared for the dark, long days and nights of struggle ahead.

This shackling of independent, creative Caribbean thought has, of course, been met with resistance particularly in recent times consequent upon the emergence of competing poles of economic and political power internationally and the financial meltdown and economic recession, erupting in September 2008, and continuing, in the citadels of world capitalism. All of this has been occurring within the context of an all pervasive process of globalization, which contains myriad contradictions. It would have been worth hearing the insights of Gordon Lewis at this historical juncture on globalization, its discontents, and its manifestations in the political economy of our region.

But we can perhaps gauge from his body of work, the perspective from which he would have drawn initial, not complete, sustenance to address globalisation. I feel sure that he would have turned to a young

German philosopher, barely thirty years old, named Karl Marx who in the *Communist Manifesto* of 1848 wrote with much, though incomplete, prescience on globalisation:

> The Bourgeoisie cannot exist without constantly revolutionising the instruments of production, and thereby the relations of production, and with them the whole relations of society. Conservation of the old modes of production in unaltered form, was, on the contrary, the first condition of existence for all earlier industrial classes. Constant revolutionising of production, uninterrupted disturbance of all social conditions, everlasting uncertainty and agitation distinguish the bourgeois epoch from all earlier ones. All fixed frozen relations, with their train of ancient and venerable prejudices and opinions, are swept away, all new-formed ones become antiquated before they can ossify. All that is solid melts into air, all that is holy is profaned, and man is at last compelled to face, with sober senses, his real conditions of life, and his relations with his kind.

> The need for a constantly expanding market for its products chases the bourgeoisie over the whole surface of the globe. It must nestle everywhere, settle everywhere, establish connections everywhere.

> The bourgeoisie has through its exploitation of its world-market given a cosmopolitan character to production and consumption in every country. To the great chagrin of Reactionists, it has drawn from under the feet of industry the national ground on which it stood. All established national industries have been destroyed or are daily being destroyed. They are dislodged by new industries, whose introduction becomes a life and death question for all civilised nations, by industries that no longer work up indigenous raw material , but raw material drawn from the remotest zones, industries whose products are consumed, not only at home, but in every quarter of the globe. In place of the old local and national seclusion and self-sufficiency, we have intercourse in every direction, universal interdependence of nations. And as in material, so also in intellectual production. The intellectual creations of individual nations become common property.

National one-sidedness and narrow-mindedness become more and more impossible, and from the numerous national and local literatures, there arises a world literature.

The bourgeoisie, by the rapid improvement of all instruments of production, by the immensely facilitated means of communications, draws all, even the most barbarian, nations into civilisation. The cheap prices of its commodities are the heavy artillery with which it batters down on Chinese walls, with which it forces the barbarians' intensely obstinate hatred of foreigners to capitulate. It compels all nations, on pain of extinction, to adopt the bourgeois mode of production; it compels them to introduce what it calls civilisation into their midst, i.e. to become bourgeois themselves. In one word, it creates a world after its own image.

All that and more face us in the Caribbean. Two basic options face us: Surrender and Continued Underdevelopment, on the one hand; or Creative Resistance and People's Development, on the other. This latter option is the only viable one, grounded in a people-centred vision, a philosophy of social democracy applied to our Caribbean condition, a socio-cultural rubric for the further ennoblement of our Caribbean civilisation, and a package of practical policies and programmes in the interest of our nations, region, and peoples.

I have outlined in my writings in recent years the case and framework for Creative Resistance and People's Development. These offerings have covered discourses on a range of matters including: globalization; the region's political economy; job creation and wealth creation; poverty reduction; the Education Revolution; the Wellness Revolution; the fight against crime; the role of the State in the development process; the quest to build a modern post-colonial economy; the impact of the revolution in information communication technology; regional integration; the existential threat of climate change; and an independent, pragmatic, productive foreign policy. The *Manifesto* and other Party documents of the political party which I have the honour to lead, the Unity Labour Party of St. Vincent and the Grenadines, are replete with an array of practical, relevant policies and programmes to effect real change for the better in people's lives. After all, that is the fundamental reason for our political engagement.

Leadership of this Creative Resistance and the Quest for overall People's Development is vital. In *The Black Jacobies*, C.L.R. James had correctly observed that great leaders make history but only to the extent that history permits them. Lewis shared this view. This was, or is, not a down-grading on leadership; rather, it was/is an extolling of a requisite leadership fit for the purpose, but nevertheless constrained, and shaped, by social forces and historical circumstances. To resist creatively the ravages of a rampant of globalisation while at the same time taking advantage of its positive, progressive features for people's development, demands, among other things, a leadership which not only instils in the people that which is good, but more importantly draws out of them that which is good and noble and to do so even when the people themselves do not as yet realise their own goodness and nobility. This intimate, and many-layered, connection between leadership and the people in a participatory setting of good governance is at the core of driving the quest for Creative Resistance and People's Development.

Walter Rodney taught us all this very well, too, in *How Europe Underdeveloped Africa*. This path-breaking book was published in 1973. At the time of its publication, the iconic Caribbean poet from St. Vincent and the Grenadines, Ellsworth "Shake" Keane, penned in celebration of Walter Rodney an apt masterpiece entitled "Private Prayer":

> To understand
> How the whole thing run
> I have to ask my parents
> And even my daughter and son
>
> To understand the form
> Of compromise I am
> I must in my own voice ask
> How the whole thing run
>
> To ask
> Why I don't dream
> In the same language I live in
> I must rise up
> Among syllables of my parents
> In the land which I am

And form
A whole daughter a whole son
Out of the compromise
Which I am

To understand history
I have to come home

To understand our Caribbean condition, and the contribution of Gordon K. Lewis to that understanding, we necessarily turn to our history and our home-coming, a coming home to ourselves. This historical reclamation and understanding provide the basis for our future, the only time, of all time, which is ours possibly to desecrate. The avoidance of this desecration and the ensuring of our people's upliftment are at the centre of our embrace of our tomorrows with our strengths and possibilities.

3.

Leadership and our Cricketing Culture: Frank Worrell and the Contemporary Caribbean

The 17ᵗʰ Sir Frank Worrell Memorial Lecture delivered at Cave Hill, University of the West Indies on July 19, 2012

Author's Note

Having been asked to deliver the 17ᵗʰ Sir Frank Worrell Memorial Lecture, I decided to write a much more extensive paper than what would normally suffice for a normal lecture. I thought that it would be useful to prepare a monograph on our cricketing culture, Sir Frank, his leadership and some of the implications for the contemporary Caribbean. I hope that this publication would be of interest to general readers but more especially young cricketers and, perhaps, administrators.

I thank Sir Hilary Beckles, Principal of the University of the West Indies, Cave Hill, Barbados for his kind invitation to deliver the lecture. I am indebted, too, to an audience of the highest quality who participated in the discussions following my presentation.

The Back-Drop: Some Relevant Facts On Frank Worrell

It is always sensible when discussing cricket and cricketers and their location in society's evolution to start with relevant facts, unvarnished and truthful. This is especially important in our instant exercise since in this subject area there has often been so much stylising of facts in search of theories of exploration. So, we begin!

Frank Mortimer Maglinne Worrell was born in Bridgetown, Barbados, in August, 1924 and died on March 13, 1967, in Jamaica, at the age of 43 years. Please note that he was born in colonial Barbados, ninety years after the Proclamation by the British Parliament which formally ended slavery in the British Caribbean; and he died four and one-half years after Jamaica and Trinidad and Tobago attained constitutional independence; less than one year, too, after Barbados' Independence. I shall return to these historical contexts later.

The basic data of Frank Worrell's cricketing career are well known. At the age of 13 years he was promoted to the first team of Combermere School. This meant that at this tender age he was participating in First Division Cricket in Barbados against a host of mature players including those who were representing or had represented Barbados in inter-territorial cricket and the West Indies in Test Cricket.

At first Worrell played for Combermere as a slow left-arm bowler and a number ten batsman. In January 1942, not yet 18 years of age, he made his debut for Barbados against Trinidad as a slow bowler who batted at number 11! As a bowler, he announced himself by taking six wickets in the match for 128 runs, off 19 overs; Trinidad scored 526 runs in the aggregate in both innings. Five of his six wickets were of batsmen in top half of the batting order: V. H. Stollmeyer, Gerry Gomez, R. P. Tang Choon, P. E. Burke, and N. S. Asgarali. Worrell's closest bowling competitor on the Barbados team was the experienced Barbados and West Indies medium-pacer, E. A. V. Williams, who also garnered six wickets in the match for 128 runs, but four of Williams' six scalps were in the lower half of Trinidad's batting order. Batting at number 11, Worrell scored 29 runs in Barbados' first innings. Clearly, he had a commendable debut.

In the second match against Trinidad, he was promoted to bat at number 10 and scored 34 not out in the first innings. In the third match against Trinidad in 1942, he was further promoted to bat at number 9 and scored 48 runs; and then went up the order to bat at number 8 in the fourth inter-territorial game against Trinidad in 1942. By 1943, he was established as an all-rounder: In the first match against Trinidad he batted at number 6, scoring 64 runs (not out) in the first innings; in the next match a few days later in Trinidad, Worrell was retained at number 6 and scored his first inter-territorial century, 188 runs in the first innings and 68 runs in the second innings against a strong bowling attack which included West Indian pacers Lance Pierre and Prior Jones and the experienced medium-pacer, the test cricketing star, Gerry Gomez.

In 1944, Barbados promoted Worrell to bat at number 4. In that batting position in February 1944 against Trinidad at Kensington Oval, Barbados, he scored his first triple century (308, not out). John Goddard batting at number 5 scored 218 not out. The Worrell-Goddard partnership was a whopping 502 runs, undefeated! Less than a week before, again against Trinidad, Worrell had bowled Barbados to victory with a nine-wicket haul in the match for a paltry 64 runs, off 20 overs, against a strong batting side which included Andy Ganteume, Jeffrey Stollmeyer, H. J. B. Burnette, Gerry Gomez, James E. D. Sealey, and R. P. Tang Choon. Worrell was not yet 19 years old when he was chalking up these epic achievements.

It is not the first time that young people, historically, had mesmerised human civilisation: At the age of 22, Alexander the Great has crossed Ilyssus, razed the city of Thebes to the ground, and brought the entire Persian Empire under his sway; at 23, Descartes evolved a new system of philosophy; at 24, William Pitt became Prime Minister of Britain, over whose empire and realms the sun was never to set; and at 25 Napoleon Bonaparte saved the Republic of France with men, gunshots and swords on the streets of Paris.

Worrell's evolution as a top class batsman was remarkable. When he made his debut in January 1942 against Trinidad batting at number 11, Clyde Walcott, also a debutante, was opening the batting for Barbados. The third of the famous three Ws, Everton Weekes, was to have his first inter-territorial game in February 1945 against Trinidad batting at number 6. Within one week thereof, the formidable trio were at numbers 2, 3, and 4. It was inevitable that opponents would suffer harshly at the hands of these batting geniuses. In February 1946, Trinidad was to be the victim at the Queen's Park Oval in Trinidad. Batting at number 4, Walcott scored an undefeated 314 runs and Worrell, 255 not out, batting at number 5, in an unbroken record partnership of 574 runs. Worrell was not yet 22 years old and Walcott was barely 20 years old. Meanwhile, Everton Weekes was scoring prolifically.

Inexorably, test cricket beckoned. Before Worrell's emergence in cricket for Barbados, the last test match which the West Indies had played was the third test against England, at Kensington Oval (London) in August 1939, the very month and year when the Second World War started. The War ended in May 1945. In 1947-1948 England toured the West Indies. Walcott and Weekes made their test debut in the first test of that series at Kensington Oval (Barbados); Worrell was not available until the second test of that series. Worrell's test debut came in February 1948, in Trinidad against England. Weekes batted at number 3, Worrell at number 4, and Walcott at number 5. Worrell made 97 in the first innings and 28 not out in the second innings in a drawn match. He took one wicket for 85 runs off 37 overs. His batting arrival had been announced in test cricket at the age of 24 years. In March 1948, he scored his first test century (131 not out) in the West Indies victory over England at Bourda, Guyana; he was the first of the 3 Ws to do so.

Between 1948 and 1963, when he retired from test cricket at the age of 39 years, Worrell played in 51 tests in 11 test series. His batting performance in 87 innings was excellent: nine 100s, twenty-two 50s, and an average of 49.48 runs per innings with a highest score of 261. In his 11 test series he topped the batting averages for the West Indies in three of them and was second in another three. He was the top batsman in the tests in England's tour of the West Indies in 1947-1948, the West Indies tour of England in 1950, and India's tour of the West Indies in 1962, at the age of 38 years. He was second in the test batting averages in the West Indies tour of Australia in 1951-1952, in the West Indies tour of England in 1957, and in England's tour of the West Indies in 1960.

Worrell's test bowling average is commendable: He bowled 7, 141 balls for 69 wickets at 38.72 runs apiece. He did so as a slow left-armer, and as a medium pacer, who often opened the bowling for the West Indies. He had two five-wicket and two four wicket hauls in test cricket. His best bowling performance was 7 wickets for 70 runs against England at Leeds in 1957.

Worrell was a remarkable all-rounder, arguably the best the West Indies has ever produced after the incomparable Garfield Sobers. A highlight of some of Worrell's all-round feats in this regard include the following: In the second test against England at Lord's in 1950 he batted at number 3 and opened the bowling with Prior Jones; in the third test of the English tour in 1950, he scored 261 runs batting at number 4 and then proceeded to open the bowling with a tight 19 overs (8 maidens) for 30 runs. In the fourth test of that series at Kennington Oval (London) he scored 138 runs batting at number 3, then opened the bowling (20 overs, 9 maidens, 30 runs), paving the way for the spin twins, Sonny Ramadhin and Alf Valentine, to share 14 wickets between them as England fell to defeat by an innings and 56 runs. In July 1957, at Headingley, Leeds, Worrell's opening of the batting and bowling for the West Indies was dramatic in a losing cause against England. The West Indies batted first with Worrell and Sobers as openers. The West Indies were bowled out for a paltry 142: Worrell got 29 runs; only Kanhai with 47 and Walcott with 38 got more than him. When England batted, Worrell took the new ball and bowled 38.2 overs (9 maidens) for 70 runs, seven wickets — his best bowling performance ever. England was bowled out for 279 runs. Immediately, Worrell was enjoined to open the West Indies' second innings. He fell for seven runs, playing a tired shot. The West Indies were bowled out for a meager 132 runs and lost by an innings and five runs.

This pattern of Worrell's going to bat early and bowl early in an innings was to recur over the years until India's tour of the West Indies in 1962 when the batting line-up was star-studded and reliable with Conrad Hunte, Rohan Kanhai, Sobers, and Joe Solomon and the bowling was gifted with Wesley Hall, Chester Watson, Charlie Stayers, Lester King, Sobers, and Lance Gibbs. The awesome Charlie Griffith was to join the fast bowling stable in 1963. Further, by 1962, Worrell was 38 years old.

Let us examine Worrell's all-round performance in the West Indies' epic tour of Australia in 1960–1961. When the first of that five-test series began in December 1960, Worrell was over 36 years old. In the West Indies batting averages for the tests, Worrell was fifth with an average of 37.50 runs over 10 innings with a highest score of 82 runs. Ahead of him were the batting revelation of the wicketkeeper batsman Franz "Gerry" Alexander (an average of 60.50 runs); R. B. Kanhai, batting at number 3 (average of 50.3 runs); G. S. Sobers, batting at number 4, (average of 43.0 runs); and the talented and experienced opening batsman, Conrad Hunte (average of 37.70 runs). Other specialist batsmen who had four or more innings namely, Seymour Nurse, Joe Solomon, Cammie Smith and Peter Lashley, were below Worrell in the batting averages.

In the bowling department on the tour of Australia (1960–1961), only Lance Gibbs and Wesley Hall topped Worrell in the West Indies test bowling averages. Gibbs took 19 wickets from 192.2 overs (65 maidens) at 20.78 runs apiece; Wesley Hall grabbed 21 wickets from 134 overs (34 maidens) at 35.7 runs apiece. Valentine, Sobers and Rahadhin were below Worrell in the bowling averages. Worrell bowled tightly with 24.5% of his overs being maidens; only Gibbs bowled more maidens (35.8%). Overall, too, Gibbs was the only bowler more economical: 192.2 eight-ball overs by him yielded just over 2 runs per over (395 runs in the aggregate) compared to Worrell's yield of 2.66 runs per eight-ball over (357 runs in 134 overs). In all this, though, we must remember that Worrell batted at number 5 in eight of his ten test innings and at number 6 in the other two. And he opened the bowling with Wesley Hall in four of the five test matches. Moreover, he was captain. All of this effort beyond his 36th year. Absolutely incredible! A leader must always be prepared to go a distance beyond that even required of his troops!

Let us delve a little more into the heroics of Worrell's individual cricket performance on that 1960-1961 tour of Australia. We shall come to his captaincy, his leadership, a little later. In the first test, the "Tied Test", he scored 65 runs in each innings and opened the bowling in each innings; he bowled 46 eight-ball overs; in the third test, which the West Indies won, he made 82 runs in the second innings, but bowled very little because of the rampaging Gibbs and Valentine; and in the dramatically drawn fourth test he made 71 and 53 runs in each of the innings and bowled 24 overs (9 maidens), and took four wickets for 61 runs.

Against India on their tour of the West Indies in 1962, nearing 38 years old, Worrell topped the West Indies' test batting averages with 88.0 runs over six innings (10 tests) with a highest score of 98 not out in the West Indies 10-wicket victory at Sabina Park, Jamaica. He batted mainly between numbers 5 and 7 in the batting order. He topped the batting averages over the outstanding batsmen, Kanhai, Sobers, Solomon and Hunte, and capable players such as Easton Mc Morris and wicket-keeper batsman Ivor Mendonca. In this 1962 West Indies-India series he bowled only 69 overs (121 runs, 2 wickets).

In Worrell's last hurrah as a test player, the West Indies tour of England in 1963, he was sixth in the West Indies' test batting averages with 20.28 runs average in eight innings and a highest score of 74 not out. He was fifth in the test bowling averages for the West Indies: 3 wickets at 34.66 apiece over 45 overs (16 maidens). Conrad Hunte, Rohan Kanhai, Basil Butcher and Garfield Sobers all had test batting averages in this 1963 series ranging from 40.25 runs to 58.87 runs. Joe Solomon was fifth in these averages with 25.50 runs. In the West Indies test bowling averages Charlie Griffith, Lance Gibbs, Garfield Sobers, and Wesley Hall were outstanding. Worrell was thus not required to bowl much on his final tour.

Worrell's all-round cricket was bolstered, too, by his excellent fielding; in his 51 tests he took 43 catches and dropped very few.

Of Worrell's eleven test series, six were against England, three against Australia, and two against India. Over his fifteen years of test cricket for the West Indies, due to various reasons, he did not tour India (1948 -1949 and 1958-1959) nor New Zealand in 1956. He did not play, too, for the West Indies against Pakistan on the latter's tour of 1958. However, Worrell did tour India with a Commonwealth XI, in the months following the 1949 West Indies tour of India. He scored 684 runs in the unofficial tests for an average of 97.71 with two centuries, including an acknowledged masterpiece of 233 not out at Kanpur. On that tour he took over as captain when the substantive captain, Les Ames, fell ill.

For completeness, the records show Worrell's batting in first class matches as follows: 208 matches; 326 innings; 49 not outs; 15,025 runs scored; highest score, 308; batting average, 54.24 runs. His first class bowling statistics are as follows: 208 matches; 26,740 balls; 10,115 runs; 349 wickets; best bowling in an innings, 7 for 70; average runs for each wicket, 28.98; 5 wickets taken thirteen times; economy rate of 2.26 runs per over. In first class matches Worrell took 139 catches.

In 2009, the influential British cricket journalist, Christopher Martin-Jenkins, authored a book entitled *The Top 100 Cricketers of All Time.* He listed Frank Worrell at number 39. Ahead of him from the West Indies were six players: Garfield Sobers (Number 3), Viv Richards (Number 9), Malcolm Marshall (Number 11), George Headley (Number 20), Brian Lara (Number 24), and Everton Weekes (Number 32). These rankings are always problematic partly because the criteria are difficult to pin down and partly due to a heavy dose of subjectivity. I feel sure, however, that Worrell ought to have been far more-highly placed given some names from England, Australia, South Africa, India, and Pakistan who were ranked ahead of him. Still, a ranking of number 39 of all-time greats is highly commendable.

Worrell captained the West Indies in three test series with an aggregate of 15 tests. The West Indies won nine tests, drew two, tied one, and lost three. In the process the West Indies won test series against England (three-to-one with one draw) and India whom they beat five-nil. Worrell's team narrowly lost two-one to Australia with one match drawn and another tied. By 1963, he had built the West Indies into, arguably, the champion side in the world. This was undoubtedly affirmed in 1965 when the touring Australians were soundly defeated in the West Indies by the team Worrell had fashioned but captained by Sobers with Worrell as Manager.

Assessing Worrell's Cricket

So far I have addressed the raw data of Worrell's performance as a cricketer, moreso a test cricketer. Some qualitative assessments are in order, particularly since the statistics do not reveal the full truth of this cricketing titan.

Let us listen to those who knew his cricketing qualities better than most to enlighten us.

First, Clyde Walcott in his book *Sixty Years on the Back Foot*, published in 1999, offers this verdict:

> As a batsman, Frank was all elegance and style. He stroked the ball just hard enough to reach the boundary whereas I would drive it with more power. He appealed more to the connoisseurs. I was involved in many big stands with him, including our world-record fourth-wicket stand of 574 in Port of Spain in 1946, and enjoyed batting with him. His mastery made it easier for whoever was batting with him. He was invariably modest about his achievements, saying after the record stand, 'the conditions were loaded in our favour. I wasn't all that delighted about it.'

> ...Summing up, I think I can say that Everton (Weekes) was the best batsman of the trio (Worrell, Weekes, Walcott), Frank (Worrell) was the best all-rounder and I was the best wicket-keeper – batsman who bowled a bit.

Second, Everton Weekes in his fascinating book *Mastering the Craft: Ten Years of Weekes, 1948–1958*, published in 2007, asserted:

> It was always a great pleasure batting with Frank (Worrell) and Clyde (Walcott). It was easier to get runs batting with Clyde because Frank's style was rather similar to my own. Sometimes the field placing, because of Clyde's ability to hit hard to mid-off and mid-on, and over extra-cover, allowed me to take advantage of openings....

> ...Frank was more like Lara, maybe slightly more delicate. He would push the ball with perfect timing pass mid-off and extra cover".

Garfield Sobers' judgment of Worrell's batting is interesting and nuanced. In his autobiography titled simply *Garfield Sobers* and published in 2002, Sobers asserted:

> Frank (Worrell) was undoubtedly a great player but between the three of them (Worrell, Weekes and Walcott), I reckon Everton (Weekes) was marginally the best. Frank has always been described as elegant, beautiful and very controlled but he

was never comfortable with the short-pitched delivery, the quick bouncer. Anything medium-paced and just above, he was at home with and would punish, but the really quick stuff from the highest quality fast bowler on a bouncy pitch would cause him difficulties. This doesn't mean he wasn't brave. He once said to me that he didn't mind how fast they bowled at him.... He was very calculating and could read a match and bat on all types of wickets.

Worrell's silky-smooth batting and exquisite timing, like Beres Hammond's soothing and exciting vocal rendition of reggae, is legendary. Michael Manley, cricket enthusiast and former Prime Minister of Jamaica, in a beautiful essay entitled "Sir Frank Worrell, Cricket and West Indian Society" recounted an animated conversation on the subject of batting between Weekes and Worrell on the 1950 West Indies tour of England. Weekes had been subjecting the English country bowlers to repeated blistering attacks at Cambridge, Essex, Nottingham and Surrey. Worrell with wit and wisdom said to Weekes: "Everton, you hit the ball too hard." Everton reacted with a certain irritation and asked: "Why?" To this Worrell intoned: "Hit it a little less hard, so the fielders will have to chase it; then they will get tired." Weekes was bemused. There is no evidence that he ever took Worrell's advice seriously!

In 1950, the West Indies scored an historic victory over England at Lord's in the second test by a huge margin of 326 runs. With the bat, Worrell contributed 52 runs in the first innings and 45 in the second innings. In the first innings for the West Indies, Allan Rae made 106 runs and Weekes, 63. In the West Indians' second innings, Walcott made 168 runs, not out, and Gomez, 70. Still, the doyen of cricket writers, Neville Cardus, was moved to write of no one but Worrell in the following terms: "An inning by Worrell knows no dawn, it begins at high noon."

In 1950, in Worrell's first overseas test tour, and the West Indies' first test series win against England in England, he was their most successful batsman in the tests with an aggregate of 539 runs and an average of 89.83 runs for each of his six innings. His batting prowess in this series earned him the accolade of one of the Wisden's "Five Cricketers of the Year" in 1951. Wisden's editor wrote:

It was the batting which drew the crowds. Even on bad pitches they (the West Indies) were superior to their opponents and were always a pleasure to watch. The three coloured players from the tiny island of Barbados stood out in a class of their own, scoring 20 centuries between them. For beauty of stroke no one in the history of the game can have excelled Worrell.

In January 1961, at the Sydney Cricket Ground, the touring West Indies team triumphed over the Australians by 222 runs. In the tourist's second innings Worrell made 82 runs to assist in chalking up the victory.

Gerry Alexander, the wicketkeeper-batsman, made 108 for the West Indies. Yet, the veteran cricketing journalist A. G. Moyes singled out Worrell's innings, thus:

> Worrell's was a lovely innings. He seemed all the time to know exactly where he wanted to hit the ball and appeared able always to guide it through the gaps in the field. Technically, he was the finest player in the West Indies and in this innings, he simply could not be faulted. If ever a man deserved a century it was Worrell that day, for he entered the arena when three (Hunte, Kanhai and Sobers) had fallen for 22, (through Allan Davidson's pace bowling), and right from the start he batted with a superb mastery that reduced Davidson in a couple of overs to mediocrity.

I think that is enough for us to appreciate, in this memorial, the extraordinary batting, and all-round cricketing, skills of the man, Her Majesty Queen Elizabeth II, knighted in 1964 as Sir Frank Worrell for services to cricket. At his death a memorial service was held for him at Westminster Abbey, Britain. At home in Barbados the outpouring of grief at his funeral was overwhelming. An extraordinary human being had left us.

The Nexus Between Cricket, Its Culture, and the Imperial Project in the Caribbean

The External Context (18th and 19th Centuries)

Cricket is the first organised team sport which the English ruling class and their upper class allies fashioned and in which they participated fully; at least the first team sport in which they took part on foot, rather than on horseback. They have supported and patronised other team sports such as football, rugby, lawn tennis and other modern spectator games but they played cricket.

The game of cricket evolved in 18th century England. In 1744, the first full "Laws of Cricket" were issued and published by 'the London Club' whose president was Frederick Louis, Prince of Wales, the father of King George III. Playing cricket was part of Frederick's English pretensions. He was after all German-born. Poor fellow, he died in 1751 after being struck by a cricket ball.

Over time "the Laws of Cricket" were altered to accommodate changes in the game. But a few core features remained constant: the pitch of 22 yards (never in metric measurement despite European Union rules); the umpires' decisions are final; the game be played on open, uncovered greens and subjected to the vagaries of the weather; the batsman be given the benefit of the reasonable doubt in any adjudication process; and a quest, however unevenly pursued, to apply a "code of gentlemanly conduct" for all its participants.

By the early 19th century, the ordinary English people absorbed cricket, its myths, and verities. In an impressive book entitled *Anyone But England: Cricket and the National Malaise* published in 1994, its author, an American political journalist who fell in love with cricket, Mike Marquesee, insisted that:

> Cricket brought the rulers into contact with a cross-section of the ruled, but it allowed them to make this contact within a circumscribed social space, the space of the cricket field, under carefully controlled conditions, embodied in the Laws of Cricket, like the common laws of property prevailing throughout the market economy. It allowed the rulers to participate in sport with others without jeopardising their social standing. Whatever happened on the field, social distinctions were preserved off it.

This dialectic of participation and separation, togetherness and divisiveness, harmony and tension in cricket and between it and stratified society became, in short order, infused with an ideology of the justness and permanence of a pre-ordained, or ordained, unchangeable social hierarchy in human affairs. It is this ideological infusion which no doubt prompted the liberal historian G. M. Trevelyan to quip that: "If the French noblesse had been capable of playing cricket with their peasants their chateaux would never have been burnt". Trevelyan's *English Social History*, published during the Second World War, served, in part, the ideological purpose of engendering British and Commonwealth unity in the battle against European fascism. His rose-tinted version of village cricket in a nostalgic countryside was that of "squire, farmer, blacksmith and labourer, with their women and children……were at ease together and happy all summer afternoon."

This stylised and idyllic view of the English countryside was advertised, wrongly, indeed preposterously even, in the aftermath of the general strike of 1926, the growing attraction of the labour movement and socialism for the British people, and the increasing strength of the British Labour Party which was part of the "unity government" in the war years and which immediately after the Second World War was voted into office in preference to the socio-economic anachronisms of Winston Churchill's Tories. The ideology of dominance, intertwined with core cricket values of pastoral peace on the village green, pretended as though the industrial revolution did not happen and that mercantile capitalism, which had defeated feudalism, had not evolved into an aggressive industrial capitalism in quest of markets and territories overseas.

Still, the phenomenal socio-economic and consequential political changes wrought in Britain's eighteenth and nineteenth centuries did not destroy the "old order". Indeed, "the old" and "the new" jostled for suzerainty and accommodated each other through the workings of the deadweight of history and the fearfulness of disorder constrained, in part, by the small geographic space of the islandness of the British Isles.

So, the settlement of 1688 and the enthronement of peculiarly Hobbesian values, embedded in John Locke's Second Treaties on Civil Government of that very year, allowed for a Leviathan through the back-door, not the front-door. Thus, a constitutional monarchy evolved. Gradually, too, the franchise was extended, bit by bit, to ground a popularly elected government, first to accommodate the burghers – the bourgeoisie – then the middle class and the working people, and, in the 20th century, the women.

Walter Bagehot, the keen observer of things socio-political and constitutional, was to write in his *English Constitution*, published in 1867, at a time of the popular explosion of cricket at home and in the colonies, of the monarchy and the British people as follows:

> ...We have whole classes unable to comprehend the idea of a constitution — unable to feel the least attachment to impersonal laws. Most do indeed vaguely know that there are some other institutions besides the Queen, and some rules by which she governs. But a vast number like their minds to dwell more upon her than on anything else, and therefore she is inestimable. A Republic has only difficult ideas in government; a Constitutional Monarchy has an easy idea too; it has a comprehensible element for the vacant many, as well as complex laws and notions for the inquiring few.

The monarchy was the aloof, celestial splendor on earth; Anglicanism was the religion; cricket, the cult; Lord's cricket ground was the temporal cathedral; Wisdem Cricket Almanack was to become the bible of the cult; the universities at Oxford and Cambridge were to churn out the ruling-class functionaries, colonial governors and administrators, who had imbibed the astonishing wine of the cricket code and packaged it for export to the colonies. This institutional and ideological superstructure was always buttressed by the Royal Navy and the Armed Forces of the British state which was in service of imperial capitalism overseas. It was a well-constructed bundle of state apparatuses, fit for the purpose.

With extraordinary gumption and patriotic chest-thumping, they swiftly popularised in the 1800s in the West Indies, and elsewhere, two anthems, the first written in the 17th century, the second in 1740:

> God save our gracious king/queen,
> Long live our noble king/queen,
> God save the king/queen!

Send him/her victorious,
Happy and glorious,
Long to reign over us;
God save the king/queen.

When Britain first, at heaven's command,
Arose from out the azure main,
This was the charter of the land,
And guardian angels sung this strain:

Rule, Britannia, rule the waves;
Britons never will be slaves.

Even today, some independent countries in the West Indies with the British sovereign as their monarch, endure the pain of hearing their Police Bands play these anthems on the ceremonial occasion of the Queen's Birthday Parade! One requires an amazing grace to cope with this!

A few years before Bagehot, the German philosopher and revolutionary, Karl Marx, then permanently resident in Britain, was to ridicule Britain's unwritten constitution as "an antiquated, obsolete, out-of-date compromise between the bourgeoisie, which rules not officially, but in fact in all spheres of civil society, and the landed aristocracy which governs officially." So, in the incisive language of Marx, the bourgeoisie ruled in fact but unofficially and the landed gentry governed officially. In cricket, of course, the landed gentry, the old aristocracy, both ruled and governed. The bourgeoisie accommodated themselves to this condition. So long as cricket assisted in maintaining social order, challenged not the bourgeoisie's 'de facto' rulership, and facilitated their expansion overseas for lands, subject peoples, and markets, all was pretty well with the new rich and their modern capitalism.

By the 1850s, in Britain, banking capital was merging inexorably with industrial capital to create an expansionist finance capital for overseas domination. In the 16th, 17th and 18th centuries, mercantile capitalism had embraced the enslavement of Africans to provide cheap labour for conquered lands in the New World, including the Caribbean. By the early 19th century, as Eric Williams teaches us in *Capitalism and Slavery*, the slave mode of economic organisation became a brake on the further expansion of industrial capitalism. Slavery had to go. Slave rebellions and revolution and the abolitionists' agitation accelerated slavery's end. But the "hinterland of exploitation" in overseas territories was vital for the further expansion of capitalism overseas in colonial and imperial garb.

As Britain's expansion overseas grew to undergird and strengthen this runaway capitalism, its ruling and governing classes further elaborated their ideological superstructure of dominance. Central to this ideological engineering were Anglicanism, Britishness, and Cricket — a veritable ABC of colonialism and imperialism. "Britishness" involved a sense of superiority, including racial superiority; a way of life worthy of imitation and emulation; the inferiority of subject peoples and their unfitness for self-government. Underpinning all this was the export of capital, technology, and coercion by the State.

Let us get a good idea what the ABC ideology superstructure was designed to protect. There is no better observer of all this than Karl Marx. Of the earlier mercantilist or old colonial system of exploitation, Marx wrote thus in *Capital* (Volume 1, Chapter xxxi):

> The discovery of gold and silver in America, the extirpation, enslavement and entombment in mines of the aboriginal population, the beginning of the conquest and looting of the East Indies, the turning of Africa into a warren for the commercial hunting of black-skins, signalised the rosy dawn of the era of capitalist production. These idyllic proceedings are the chief momenta of primitive accumulation....

> The colonial system ripened, like a hothouse, trade and navigation... the treasures captured outside Europe by undisguised looting, enslavement and murder, floated back to the mother country and were turned into capital.

That very capital of the earlier period fuelled industrial capitalism and its expansionism overseas. Writing in 1848 in the *Manifesto of the Communist Party* of this expansionist industrial capitalism, Marx and his collaborator Friedrich Engels contended:

The bourgeoisie, by rapid improvement of all instruments of production, by the immensely facilitated means of communication, draws all, even the most barbarian nations, into civilisation. The cheap prices of its commodities are the heavy artillery with which it battens down all Chinese walls, with which it forces the barbarians' intensely obstinate hatred of foreigners to capitulate.... Just as it has made the country dependent on the towns, so it has made barbarian and semi-barbarian countries dependent on the civilised ones, nations of peasants on nations of bourgeois, the East on the West.

It is true that in the last quarter of the 19th century, Britain lost industrial supremacy, first to the United States of America and then, for a while, to Germany. But Britain still led the way in the export of capital and colonial expansion. The export and consolidation of cricket in the colonies was part of the supporting ideological superstructure for expanding capitalism and colonialism.

Britain's territorial expansion overseas was awesome. Between 1884 and 1900 Britain acquired 3.7 million square miles of new colonial territories. By 1914, the British Empire covered 12.7 million square miles, of which the United Kingdom represented 121,000 square miles or less than one-hundredth part, the self-governing Dominions seven million square miles, and the colonial or dependent empire 5.6 million square miles, or forty-six times the area of the United Kingdom. The population totaled 431 millions, of which the white self-governing population of Britain and the Dominions totaled 60 million, or under one-seventh. During the 1914-18 World War, Britain acquired a further 1.5 million square miles of territory. R. Palme Dutte in *The Crisis of Britain and the British Empire*, published in 1953, tells us that "By the eve of the Second World War the British Empire, protectorates and dependencies covered one-quarter of the earth's surface and one-quarter of the world's population."

While Britain was pillaging, robbing, and killing colonial peoples overseas, its ideology of dominance, inclusive of a cricketing culture, was being hypocritically elaborated and fine-tuned. Marquesee educates us as follows:

In 1867, Lillywhite advised young cricketers, 'Do not ask the umpire unless you think the batsman is out; it is not cricket to keep asking the umpire questions.' The 'cricket' in 'it is not cricket' had come to refer to a transcendent code of behaviour above and beyond the explicit laws of the game. By the end of the end of the century 'it isn't cricket' was being widely applied to all spheres of public and private life. On the eve of World War I, Lord Harris staked the boldest of claims for cricket: 'It is an institution, a passion, one might say a religion. It has got into the blood of the nation, and wherever British men and women are gathered together there will the stumps be pitched'.

The colonial administrators, Governors and Viceroys who manned the British territorial outposts overseas were schooled in this ethos and value system of cricket to serve Britain's imperialism. *Tom Brown's Schooldays* authored by Thomas Hughes (Rugby and Oxford), parliamentarian, barrister, and cricketer, groomed the young men of the ruling and governing classes accordingly:

> It's more than a game. It's an institution', said Tom. "Yes" said Arthur, "the birthright of British boys, old and young, as *habeas corpus* and trial by jury are to British men.

Around the same time, John Stuart Mill, the darling of British liberalism, was enthralling the world with his books on *Liberty* and on *Representative Government*. These political virtues he insisted were available for 'civilised' peoples like the British but not for subject peoples who were as yet not fit to receive these blessings of liberty and representative government. We still hear echoes of these untenable propositions around the globe today. To be properly prepared for self-government, the "natives" in the West Indies, among other things, apparently had to embrace and play cricket more than a little while longer.

Cricket as Liberation, Accommodation and Community in the West Indies

How is it then that this very English game, developed and led by aristocrats of the governing class in imperial Britain, associated with myths of English superiority, and a buttressing pillar of Britain's ideology of dominance, became so popular, national and liberating in colonial West Indies? How did a core superstructural feature of colonial socialisation become a tool of national liberation and acquired a permanence in the psychological make-up and popular culture of former colonies in the West Indies?

Hilary Beckles assists us in unraveling these complexities and contradictions in an introductory essay to his *Development of West Indies Cricket (Volume 1): The Age of Nationalism.* Permit me to quote him, approvingly, at length:

> Dialectical analysis best explains the dichotomous development of social culture of West Indies Cricket. The elite colonial community saw in cricket a zone of exclusive cultural activity consistent with its social and ideological outlook. Blacks, Asians and other oppressed ethnic minorities — the Chinese in particular — in turn saw this space as one on which they could gradually encroach without incurring severe penalties, but at the same time promote actions of a powerful symbolic nature designed to further the cause of the democratic revolution initiated by anti-slavery legislation.

> West Indies cricket, therefore, was born, raised and socialized within the fiery cauldron of colonial oppression and social protest. In its mature form it is essentially an ideological and politicised species and knows no world better than that of liberation struggle....

> The imported brand of Victorian cricket was transformed into a vehicle of the nascent democratising national order. The infusion into its core values of a range of subaltern expressions and expectations resulted in the 'carnivalisation' of crowd responses, which in turn became a barometer of political consciousness and a

promoter of anti-systemic ideology. The text offers a sociological comment on the process whereby cricket was creolized, politcised, and ritualised within the context of the region's radical anti-colonial tradition.

Ethnicity and mass politics provided the social and ideological mechanics of Caribbean race relations and determined the manner in which the cricket culture, already a carrier of imperialistic attitudes and values about 'natives', was further transformed by ideologies found 'beyond the boundary'.

Leon Trotsky, the anti-Stalinist Bolshevik and Marxist theoretician, had long ago insisted that to transform, alter significantly, or transcend the culture of an 'ancien regime', it was necessary to understand it, and even participate in its central contours, without accepting its functional premises which buttress the old order. Indeed, there is no other practical or lasting way. The cultural forms of a dying or decaying social order contain within them seeds for a new, different, and better dispensation. The context of the culture necessarily requires interrogation to uplift further the human condition, to ennoble ever more the civilisation, and to be utilised, if required, to advance political liberation. Still, cricket, which has been an instrument of liberation in the West Indies also compromised us in that very liberation or made it less harsh, more humanist. It is a complicated, dialectical matter.

The liberation and humanist dimensions of cricket are further emphasised by Tim Hector in his 1994 essay entitled "West Indian Nationhood, Interrogation and Cricket Politics":

> I am therefore making the case for cricket that it became a means, part of the process of the Caribbean humanising itself and therefore liberating itself from the physical and social shackles in which West Indian society was born and bound. Cricket in the West Indies is more than a game, more than popular art. West Indian cricket is part of the process by which West Indians overcame or sought to overcome the racism, and the consequent sense of racial inferiority and racial self-contempt in which

the great majority of us were born. It is part and parcel of the nationalist movement. West Indian cricket is part of the process of national liberation in the Caribbean.

Though much has changed enormously in West Indian cricket and society, there is still an enduring familiarity with the pre-existing conditions. Perhaps our people's acceptance of core values of the cricketing culture of fairness, equality of opportunity, justice, team solidarity, impartial decision-making by umpires (adjudicators), and popular participation, have made it easier for the populations to accept social democracy and its liberal underpinnings, 'beyond the boundary'. In the Law Courts across the West Indies one hears the common law resonance from core components of the cricketing culture: The defendant must be given the benefit of any reasonable doubt; the prosecutor must be fair in upholding the criminal code and ought not to persecute anyone; the judges are fair and impartial and their decisions final unless reversed on appeal; and decorum in the Court, as on the cricket field, is to be upheld in all circumstances.

Social democracy, liberty and representative government have altered markedly the West Indian condition consequent upon the "social democratic revolution" of the mid-1930s and thereafter. Yet peculiarly, it has all happened in the gradualist, accommodating manner of cricket. So much so that it is reminiscent of George Orwell's verdict in *The Lion and the Unicorn: Socialism and the English Genius*, first published in 1941:

> It (the revolution in England) will show a power of assimilating the past which will shock foreign observers and sometimes make them doubt whether any revolution has happened.

Of course, in the West Indies, the social democratic revolution is yet to be completed.

By the early 19th century in the West Indies cricket was blossoming. Wider acceptance of, and popular participation in, the game came into full flowering in the years following emancipation. By the late 1890s the sport was widespread throughout British colonial West Indies.

Invariably, there were several cricket grounds in the capital cities; and on each sugar plantation, of which there were many, there was a cricket field often in close proximity to a rural village or community. In the larger or more developed territories major clubs with their own cricket facility emerged such as at Sabina Park in Jamaica, Queens Park Oval in Trinidad, Bourda in British Guiana, and Kensington Oval in Barbados. These clubs played a dominant role in the organisation of cricket in their respective countries and in the wider West Indies. It was not until the late 1960s and thereafter that players from the smaller or less developed territories in the Windward and Leeward Islands got selection on a regular basis for the West Indies team, which had acquired "test" status in 1928. The administrators in the Windwards and Leewards barely had a presence in the regional, cricket architecture.

Jimmy Richards and Mervyn Wong in their magisterial volume, *Statistics of West Indies Cricket 1865–1989*, published in 1990, record that the first inter-territorial match, a two-day affair, was between Barbados and British Guiana at the Garrison Savannah, Barbados, in February 1865. Between 1865 and 1895, they catalogue eighteen cricket matches between British Guiana, Trinidad and Barbados. The first three-day game was between British Guiana and Barbados at Bourda in September 1895. In September 1896 Jamaica joined this trio of countries from the Eastern Caribbean in competitive inter-territorial matches. Between September 1896 and June 1928 when the West Indies achieved "test" status, there were 44 inter-territorial matches played between these four West Indian territories. Four-day inter-territorial matches started in 1912 but no games were played during the war years, 1914 to 1918; resumption occurred in February 1920. In the 1960s the Combined Islands (Windwards and Leewards) entered the regional competition, though they were later to play separately. Of course, there were regular intra-Windward and intra-Leeward islands matches, including those of the major boys' secondary schools. Cricket had become an integrating force regionally.

Before the turn of the 20th century, two teams visited from England: R. Slade Lucas' team which lost to a Jamaican side in 1895; and Lord Hawke's team which toured several islands in the Eastern Caribbean, including St. Vincent, in 1897–1898.

One hundred years before Lord Hawke's side visited St. Vincent, the British had been engaged in a genocidal war against the Kallinagoes (Caribs) and the Garifuna (descendents of Callinagoes and Africans). Britain had obtained suzerainty over St. Vincent (named St. Vincent and the Grenadines after independence in 1979), at the Treaty of Paris in 1763. Within one year, the British declared that all lands in St. Vincent belonged to the Crown and sent out Land Surveyors to give effect to their land grab. The Callinagoes and the Garifuna had hitherto owned in common all the land, almost 100,000 acres, in St. Vincent, save and except for two or three thousand acres on the western side of the island, occupied by some French settlers from Martinique and Guadeloupe. Not-so-generously the British denied the French of the right to own any land in fee simple and converted those holdings into leaseholds. Between 1763 and 1800, the Callinagoes and the Garifuna were driven from their lands through a succession of skirmishes, wars against the indigenous people, and illegal land seizures. By 1800, the indigenous people, genocide, forced deportations, were banished onto a mere 238 acres of the worst land in the most inhospitable part of the country, in the north-east In 1795, in the so-called Second Carib War, the British defeated the Callinagoes and Garifuna, killed the people's Chief, Joseph Chatoyer (now the Right Excellent Joseph Chatoyer, National Hero since 2002), carried out large scale genocide against the Callinagoes and Garifuna, and deported some 3,000 to Roatan Island off to the coast of Belize and Honduras. Genocide, land robbery, official violence of the colonial state, and the deprivation of 200 years ago are the durable, intractable roots of underdevelopment and poverty in St. Vincent and the Grenadines.

The cricketing culture of fairness and justice demands that reparations be paid to my country by the British for this systematic genocide and pillage. In 1763, there were just about 2,000 African slaves on the limited lands under French possession planting tobacco, pimento, cotton, spices, and ground provisions. By 1834, there were in excess of 22,000 African slaves mainly on sugar plantations owned by the British. Reparations are in order for our people's enslavement, too.

So, in 1897 when Lord Hawke's team visited St. Vincent to play cricket, the history of conquest, settlement, genocide, slavery and British colonial exploitation was not on their minds. On a matting wicket, the contest was keen. The Vincentians had a lead of thirteen runs on the first innings.

Richard Ollivierre of St. Vincent bowled Lord Hawke for a duck in the first innings. This happening caused *"the several thousand spectators to throw their hats into the air, beat the ground with their sticks, and shake hands with one another."*

In the second innings Pelham Warner and Lord Hawke counter-attacked. Warner was a Trinidadian by birth who later went on to captain England, struck a splendid 156, and Hawke reached fifty. Warner in his book *Cricket in Many Climes* described the scene vividly and the danger posed by the hefty hitting of Hawke and himself to spectators, including women who were decked out in bright, festive clothing:

> Hawke hit two colossal sixes, one of which nearly killed a lady who was watching the game from the balcony of her house. The ball struck the woodwork about a foot from her face.... I made one drive straight over the bowler's head, which knocked a tray full of cakes clean off the head of a black woman who was standing near the ropes.

Warner lamented the fact that one or two of the Vincentian batsmen seemed rather disinclined to go when they were given out by the umpire. The fullness of the cricketing culture was yet to be imbibed, even though the crowd response was huge.

Warner was to observe the following when Hawke's team visited Barbados:

> The whole population was mad on cricket; and when we appeared on deck, we were summoned by an excited little crowd.... After breakfast we went on shore, where a huge swarm of black men awaited us on the wharf.... As soon as we were landed from the Gulf Steamer, we were swept down by a large gathering of black men, whose enthusiasm was simply — tropical!

By the 1890s cricket had clearly become very popular in the West Indies. Popular enthusiasm greeted Lord Hawke's team everywhere. In Grenada, "a large crowd came to see us off", and the crowd in St. Vincent "mostly black, were very enthusiastic". Still, the issue of race was very much present. Warner commented thus:

(In Trinidad and) in the smaller islands such as Grenada, St. Kitts, St. Vincent, Antigua, and St. Lucia, black men are always played... but Barbados and Demerara have strenuously set themselves against this policy. With this uncompromising attitude I cannot agree. These black men add considerably to the strength of a side, while their inclusion makes the game more popular locally, and tends to instill a mutual and universal enthusiasm among all classes of the population.

Every single book on West Indian cricket, especially those of test cricketers (Weekes, Worrell, Walcott, Stollmeyer, Hall, Lloyd, Holding, Garner, Richards, Marshall, Lara, and others), speaks to the community-based nature of the game and the impact of that community-spiritedness on their development as players and human beings. C. L. R. James' *Beyond a Boundary* (1963) is stuffed with anecdotes, facts, and analysis about this community phenomenon of West Indian cricket. Similarly, an acute observer of West Indian cricket, Clayton Goodwin, has catalogued in some detail the community-spiritedness of our cricket in his book, *West Indians at the Wicket*, published in 1986. So, too, Michael Manley's *A History of West Indies Cricket* (1988).

When I was a boy and into my teenage years (1950–1965), the community-spiritedness of village cricket had a parallel in community-based church activities. There were competitive games at all levels within my small rural village of Colonarie, and between the villages or communities across St. Vincent. This has continued up to recent times. Nowadays cross-village or community or even national clubs have, by and large, replaced the particular village or community clubs. Up to my teenage years and sometime thereafter, practically everyone was involved in the cricket clubs and matches: Teachers, the planters, businessmen, policemen, farmers, workers, the unemployed, women, the elderly, the middle-aged, and the youths. Village cricket on Saturdays or Sundays was a popular pastime. The better cricketers would sometimes play for a nation-wide club in the national competitions in the hope of selection for the national team and beyond. The community also became involved whenever the West Indies team was playing anywhere in the world. We were glued to our radios. Indeed, interest was high, too, in the regional games even when neither St. Vincent nor the Windwards Combined were playing. We listened on medium-wave radio transmissions from Barbados, Trinidad, Jamaica or Grenada.

I vividly recall, for example, such community involvement in my small rural village when the West Indies toured Australia in 1960-1961. There were two short-wave radios in my village of Colonarie — the box radios with the big tubes inside: One, a German Grundig, owned by my father and was in his retail shop; the other, a Pye or a Phillips, owned by Mr. Latham who had returned from the Dutch Antilles to which he had earlier migrated. Two groups of men and boys followed the five tests in Australia through the nights, local time, on one of these two radios. When the players went for lunch whether at Perth, Brisbane, Sydney, Adelaide or Melbourne, we would at the dead of night also eat from a group or communal cook-up, pre-arranged. One or more persons were detailed to keep scores of each day's play in an exercise book. We knew the statistics; years later I still have recall of scores and minor details of this or that test.

The series against Australia was of great interest particularly since Worrell was appointed as captain. Further, Australia was seen as the world champions. We wanted to beat them; we felt that we had the nucleus of a team to do so. Although England had won the 1959-1960 series against us in the West Indies, we thought that we had the better team, but it was not well-led. In batting we had Hunte, Kanhai, Sobers and Worrell with possible support from Joe Solomon and Seymour Nurse. In the bowling department there were Wesley Hall, Sobers, Worrell, Valentine, Ramadhin, and Lance Gibbs in the wings. Gerry Alexander was a good wicketkeeper, even though unsuitable as captain. Above all, though, we were excited that the best leader, an experienced and exceptionally wise black man, Frank Worrell was destined to lead the West Indies team into a new and better dispensation.

In my village I do not recall that we knew of C. L. R. James' campaign in the *Nation*, the newspaper of Dr. Eric Williams' People's National Movement (PNM) of Trinidad and Tobago. But we were convinced that Worrell would make a tremendous difference for the better. All around us there were quests for new and better conditions of life. In St. Vincent, Ebenezer Joshua was challenging the plantocracy and colonialism.

In Cuba, we knew that Fidel Castro was trying something new. In our underdeveloped political consciousness we were excited about the prospect of a youthful President John Kennedy in the USA and his "Camelot". Anti-colonialism was awash in Asia and Africa. Martin Luther King was striking blows for human rights and the upliftment of black people in America. And we still had faith that the West Indies Federation would survive, build us a nation, and help us improve our lives. In that context, we had an undefined expectancy of glory for the West Indies in Australia, led by the first black man ever to captain the West Indies in a test series.

Years later I was to read this insightful passage in C. L. R James' *Beyond a Boundary*:

> What do they know of cricket who only cricket know? West Indians crowding in Tests bring with them the whole past history and future hopes of the islands. English people, for example, have a conception of themselves breathed from birth. Drake and mighty Nelson, Shakespeare, Waterloo, the Charge of the Light Brigade, and the few who did so much for so many, the success of parliamentary democracy, those and such as those constitute a national tradition. Underdeveloped countries have to go back centuries to rebuild one. We of the West Indies have none at all, none we know of. To such people the three Ws, Ram and Val wrecking English batting, help to fill a huge gap in their consciousness and in their needs. In one of the sheds on the Port of Spain wharf is a painted sign: 365 Garfield Sobers. If the old Maple-Shannon-Queen's Park type of rivalry was now insignificant, a nationalist jealousy had taken its place.

When cricket came to the West Indies in the late 18th century and early nineteenth century, our societies were culturally plural in the sense that each of the racial or cultural sections had its own relatively distinct pattern of socio-cultural integration. The penetration and spread of modern capitalism, global interconnectedness, inter-racial mating, cultural creolisation in small geographic spaces, the growth of popular democracy, the growing attraction of Christianity and cricket, and the distillation and consensus of a core of values, all contributed to the evolution from a culturally plural society to an integrated whole with an admixture of heterogeneity and homogeneity. Cricket and its code of conduct, encompassing the Laws of Cricket but wider, assumed a major role in the fashioning of a more integrated and creolised society.

British administrators, the planter-merchant elite, soldiers, prelates and a black or mixed middle class contributed to the embrace and propagation of the code of cricket, interlaced as it was with an abiding hypocrisy by its propagandists. But quite important in this regard was the impact of the expatriate teachers, including headmasters, who had been trained in elite British schools. Their influence was far greater than their numbers. James is strong on this point:

> At these schools for many years there were some two hundred boys, children of Englishmen and local whites, many sons of the brown-skinned middle class, Chinese, Indians, and black boys, often poor who had won some of the very few scholarships to these schools, and others, not too many, whose parents could afford it. These Oxford and Cambridge men taught us Latin and Greek, Mathematics and English Literature, but they also taught, rather diffused, what I can only call the British public-school code.

> The success of this code inside the classrooms was uncertain. In the playing fields, especially the cricket field, it triumphed. Very rapidly we learned to 'play with the team', which meant subordinating your personal inclinations and even interests to the good of the whole. We kept a 'stiff upper lip' in that we did not complain about ill fortune. We did not denounce failure but 'well tried' or 'hard luck' came easily to our lips. We were generous to opponents and congratulated them on victories, even when we knew they did not deserve them. We absorbed the same discipline through innumerable boy's books..... Generation after generation of boys of the middle class went through this training and experience. And took it out into the West Indian world with them, the world of the games they continued to play and the world outside. The masses of the people paid little attention to this code but they knew it, and one condition of rising to a higher status in life was obedience or at least obeisance to it.

This code drawing from the foundation head of knowledge from Western civilisation, discipline and order, civility and good manners, solidarity, equality and justice, and turning setbacks into advances are all meritorious values to cultivate. Still, they have to be put in the service of the people as a whole; and the boundaries of knowledge and understanding from Western civilisation must be expanded to embrace universalism but through the prism of the real condition and values of our Caribbean civilisation. That nexus and solidarity with the mass of the people, the embrace of universalism and the particularism of our Caribbean civilisation, and the quest for our people's upliftment are the noise in our blood, the echo in our bones. The best of our cricket and our cricketers exemplify this further ennoblement of our Caribbean civilisation.

C. L. R. James subscribed to "the code" but he understood that when it stood in the way of human progress through its misuse or abuse by the reactionary planter-merchant elite, that "code" had to be turned inside out. Thus was the case in his highly successfully campaign in 1960 for Worrell to assume the captaincy of the West Indies team as the replacement for Gerry Alexander.

Distinction Style of West Indies Cricket

One aspect of our cricketing culture remains to be explored: the style and manner in which the West Indies play cricket. To be sure, as Albert Camus reminds us, "style like fine silk often hides eczema." But each people deliver their cultural outpourings with its own distinctiveness. The iconic Rex Nettleford had long identified West Indians at cricket as creative artists, performers of the creative imagination with their minds and bodies, a type of 'creative dance', so to speak. The esteemed Gladstone Mills of Jamaica, professor of public administration and cricketer, gloried in the special artistry of West Indian cricket in his *Grist for the Mills: Reflections on a Life*, published in 1994. West Indians do not play cricket with what C. L. R. James bitingly critiqued as the "welfare state of mind": dull, boring, predictable, lacking in zest, creativity, and imagination. The West Indian persona, distilled through what Derek Walcott calls, "the fever of history", is naturally joyous and serious, exhilarating and careful, enterprising yet prudent. It is not the "calypso", "soca" or "reggae" cricket of the caricature imposed by those who do not know us or have not our interest at heart. The one-sidedness of the designations by the caricaturists seeks to belittle the achievements of a region of only five million people who were world cricket champions for at least 15 years unbroken from the late 1970s onwards. Only two other nations have matched this accomplishment in sport: Cuba in the field of amateur boxing and the Soviet Union/Russia in ice hockey. Not even amazing Brazil of 195 million people were able to rule the global roost in football for 15 unbroken years!

One sympathetic foreign observer of West Indians at play in cricket, the Australian journalist Johnny Moyes had this to say in his book *With the West Indies in Australia 1960–61*:

> Those who had the pleasure of watching the West Indian cricketers in action and of knowing them personally will never forget them. The impact they made on cricket in Australia was amazing: they turned the world upside down: they arrived almost unhonoured and unsung; they took away with them the esteem, affection, and admiration of all sections of the community. They gave the genuine cricket lover a thrill he had not felt for a quarter of a century. They brought back to the grounds many who had left them in disgust at the mediocre fare served up to them. They proved what so many of us had declared — that people would go to see cricket played as a game and entertainment.

> The thrills were provided by the West Indians. No Australian during the series played with half the brilliance of Sobers at Brisbane or Kanhai at Adelaide. On these occasions these two grand players undoubtedly touched the skirts of Genius. Their stroke-play was superb; their timing precise; their placing of the ball amazing in the extreme. Except for brief outpourings by O'Neill and that dazzling opening of the second Australian innings at Melbourne by Simpson there was nothing in the Australian batting to compare with the glorious artistry so often shown by some of the West Indians, who exploded into their strokes as did the champions of other days. The West Indians

were 'different'. The Australians often scored as quickly. It was the manner in which the West Indians made their strokes that was so attractive....

This captures well West Indians at the wicket! In his book, *Beating the Field: My Own Story*, published in 1995, the world class West Indian batsman, Brian Lara, addresses "The West Indian Way", thus:

The West Indian way of playing cricket is to try to entertain, to be flamboyant and to enjoy it. From a very young age boys will be trying to improve their game on the beach or on little-used roads or bare patches of land — anywhere they can find. And they will be doing it with some style and charisma.

...Cricket was passed on to us by the plantation owners and their workers. The West Indian labourers who took it up wanted to be different in their approach to the game from the people who oppressed them, so they were much more aggressive in using their physical strength and gift of coordination between hand and eye to strike the ball great distances. Just to be allowed to play cricket in those days meant a degree of freedom for them. They were playing a sport they could enjoy and that feeling lives on.

Leadership, Worrell and the Contemporary Caribbean
Context and Text of Worrell's Leadership

I begin this section of the discourse on leadership, Worrell and the contemporary Caribbean with a lengthy quotation from Karl Marx's brilliant work entitled *The Eighteenth Brumaire of Louis Napoleon*, published in 1869:

Men make their own history, but they do not make it just as they please; they do not make it under circumstances chosen by themselves, but under circumstances directly encountered, given and transmitted from the past. The tradition of all the dead generations weighs like a nightmare on the brain of the living. And just when they seem engaged in revolutionising themselves and things, in creating something that has never yet existed, precisely in such periods of revolutionary crisis they anxiously conjure up the spirits of the past to their service and borrow from them names, battle cries and costumes in order to present the new scene of world history in this time – honoured disguise and this borrowed language.... In like manner a beginner who has learnt a new language always translates it back into his mother tongue, but he has assimilated the spirit of the new language and can fully express himself in it only when he finds his way in it without recalling the old and forgets his native tongue in the use of the new.

In *Black Jacobins*, C. L. R. James undoubtedly utilised Marx's insights in his study of the role which the revolutionary leader, Toussaint L'Ouverture, played in the Haitian Revolution towards the end of the 18th century. Let's do the same with Worrell, his leadership, and the implications for the contemporary Caribbean.

So, let us identify the relevant facts, historical circumstances, personality and behavioural traits, which helped to shape and define Worrell's cricket and leadership. Worrell was born in 1924 in a colonial Barbados ruled by an unrepresentative government locally and an imperial centre externally; universal adult suffrage was to come in 1946. In 1937, when Worrell represented Combermere School in first division cricket, the workers and other patriots of Barbados, led by Clement Payne, rose up in anti-colonial rebellion. Before universal adult suffrage, Worrell had first played for Barbados (1942), made his first century for Barbados (1943), and chalked up his first triple century (1944) in that famous territorial match against Trinidad at Kensington when he and John Goddard made the unbroken record-breaking partnership of 502. In the very year of universal adult suffrage, Worrell partnered with Walcott for another unbroken record stand of 574 against Trinidad in Port of Spain; Worrell's contribution was 255. It was as though they were heralding and celebrating the coming of one person, one vote. Two years later he made his test debut at that very ground against England. What a joinder of circumstances! Worrell personally marked the occasion with 97 runs in the West Indies' first innings and 28 not out in the second, in a drawn match.

Internal self-government was to arrive for Barbados in the 1950s and independence in 1966, three years after Worrell retired from test cricket and one year before his untimely death at 43 years of age.

For Worrell's entire life-time, the economy of Barbados was dominated by a largely white planter-merchant elite. Political economists such as Dr. Richard "Johnny" Cheltenham, and Dr. George Belle, have written compelling on this dominance and its constricting effect on Barbadian society.

The impact of race, class, and economics has been precisely and eloquently addressed by Everton Weekes in his book *Mastering the Craft:*

...In those early days (the 1940s), scoring runs was no guarantee of selection. There were lots of off the field issues that could determine selection. It took one a little time to feel secure in the Barbados and West Indies teams. There were the issues of race and class that dominated the social world of cricket. Everyone who was honest would admit this, but very few people were prepared to talk about it, or try to eradicate its power.

It was very strong in Barbados but also in Jamaica. George Headley had his troubles in the early days. He did not discuss it much but he was very aware of the nature of these things. Prior to my Test debut in 1948 a black man had never captained the West Indies side. White players like the Grant brothers from Trinidad captained Headley, men also could not try on his cricket boots.

Headley captained just one Test, the one in which I made my West Indies debut on January 1948. It was a one-off game, but during the 1930s when he carried the team on his back he was considered too black and too poor without an appropriate education. The prejudice was very intense. I was never captained by a black man in the Barbados team. When I became captain in 1960 I was the first black man to lead Barbados.

This was the racial environment in which I grew up as a national and international cricketer. It was ruled by strong racist principles and a chap, especially one like me from the working class, had to be very careful.... This was the hard reality that shaped Barbados and Caribbean society. I supposed it was the same in most institutions.

Frank Worrell was born into cricket. The house where he was born overlooked the Empire cricket ground. Clyde Walcott affirmed that Frank "took an interest in the game almost as soon as he could walk". Worrell was brought up at Bank Hall, a few hundred yards from the test ground at Kensington Oval. Walcott was born on the corner of Baxter's Road and Westbury Road, somewhat closer to Kensington in the other direction; and Weekes was born 300 yards from Kensington at Pickwick Gap. As Weekes said in his book, he was born in a "village academy" of cricket and "raised in the shadow of Kensington". So, too, Worrell and Walcott.

A little recounted fact was that Worrell and his friends had a team called the Starvation Eleven and they played cricket every day in the school holidays, each match lasting several days. Walcott insists "that is where he learned to play long innings". As Worrell himself recalled: "If we weren't in the churchyard playing cricket, we were on the beach. Our lives revolved around cricket."

Worrell attended Combermere School, one of the more prestigious secondary schools in Barbados in which devotion to cricket was almost religious. At age 13, Worrell was promoted from the fourth team to the first team at Combermere by the legendary games master, V.B. Williams. In his book *Cricket Punch*, Worrell tells the story thus:

> I enrolled at Combermere School...which meant first-class cricket in Barbados. The school teams are made up of both pupils and masters, and we had on our staff Derek Sealy...but even with a former test star on your side, it was a bit tough for a thirteen-year old boy to be playing in top-grade cricket. Nevertheless, it was a great experience. I found myself up against some of the best players in the West Indies, and there is no better way of learning than by coming up against the finest opponents.

C. L. R. James was to write of Worrell's cricketing arrival in *The Cricketer* (May 5, 1967), in an article entitled "Sir Frank Worrell: The Man Whose Leadership Made History", thus:

> Worrell was no accident. The merchant-planter class of Barbados made cricket into the popular artistic expression and social barometer of the West Indies. That was the environment which moulded the future Worrell. He was a prodigy, at the age of thirteen playing his school against cricketers like Martindale, whose pace at the time was too much for most English batsmen... Barbados selected him as a slow left-hander, but sent in as a nightwatchman, he at once earned his place as a batsman. Before he was twenty he had scored 300 runs in a first-class match. But the Barbados social discipline was very firm. Even when playing for the island as a schoolboy he had to attend school every morning until play began.

Worrell's biographer, Guyanese Ernest Eytle, in his book *Frank Worrell: The Career of a Great Cricketer*, published in 1963, informs us that Worrell was well-above average as a student but was not particularly amenable to authoritarian discipline. Indeed, he preferred to practice his cricket with his friends in a corner of the Empire ground rather than in organised practices at Combermere School; Empire's groundsman, the accommodating John Morgan, had prepared a pitch for them.

Frank Worrell loved cricket and embodied the "fairness" and "reasonable" doctrines in the cricketing culture. But he did not accept the "public school code" of cricket in all its aspects. On one occasion, his housemaster scolded him for batting on to score a double century in a house match with telling words: "Why don't you get out and give someone else a chance to bat?" On another occasion, he left a house match before the end to go to a cinema and was duly suspended. He was before his headmaster on many occasions for trifling disciplinary issues. It is evident that Worrell found many of the strictures of school authority overbearing and stifling. Undoubtedly his rapid promotion to the first team caused some resentment from his fellow-students, who were much less talented.

After leaving Combermere as a student, he joined its staff briefly as a teacher in the junior forms. He left for a stint in Trinidad but was back in Barbados shortly afterwards to work as an insurance agent. Walcott remembered him thus:

> He (Worrell) was a young man with an opinion of his own and he had strong views about what he saw as discrimination against black players when it came to the selection of sides. This sense of injustice coloured his views on life generally and turned him into a campaigner on behalf of the poor and the disadvantaged.

Worrell, intellectually sharp and curious, possessed of a sound secondary school education, brilliant at his cricket all-round, would naturally have felt constrained in colonial Barbados. He wanted more for himself, his family and community but the opportunities for advancement were limited and stultifying.

Of the situation in the late 1940s in Barbados, Weekes had this to say in *Mastering the Craft:*

> ...The society was evolving around us, and it was being said that we were witnessing a fundamental transition from the old to the new. I know a lot of people who decided to leave Barbados, disenchanted for one reason or another with the society. Some professional blacks were not prepared to live through the pain of being second class in their own country. Many packed up because of the slow pace of change.

Frank Worrell, yearning for further education, greater opportunities as a professional cricketer and a better life, left Barbados for Jamaica in 1947, shortly after his epic stand in Trinidad with Walcott. He also played professional cricket for Radcliffe in the Central Lancashire League in England, where he remained for twelve seasons from 1948 onwards. It is at Radcliffe that he developed into a wily medium-pace bowler, to supplement his left-arm spin. In his first year in the League, he took 66 wickets and averaged 88 with the bat, an outstanding performance. At Manchester University, Worrell pursued his Bachelor's degree in sociology and economics in the 1950s. He settled in Jamaica. He played cricket in Jamaica for Boys Town, a working boys club in Kingston, where he contributed immensely to youth development. After his retirement from test cricket he was made a Senator in Jamaica's Parliament and obtained employment at the University of the West Indies in a senior administrative capacity.

The story of Worrell's migration to Jamaica is interestingly told by Everton Weekes: A Mr. Vaz, a prominent industrialist and influential person in cricketing circles in Jamaica had invited Weekes in 1947 to live in, and play cricket for, Jamaica. Weekes declined the invitation because he was in the Army in Barbados. Worrell, however, took up the offer when he was told of it by Weekes.

Worrell understood migration well: When he was a boy, his father was away in the merchant service and was hardly around. His mother, a seamstress, went to live in New York, taking his brother, Livingstone with her. Like many West Indian parents, then and now, they went in search of better opportunities for themselves and their families.

Worrell was socialized in a household led by his grandmother; she instilled in him a core of sound moral values, integrity, discipline, hard-work and personal ambition, commitment to family and the community, a spirit of solidarity with the disadvantaged, an aversion to injustice and unequal treatment based on race or class, a belief in Christianity, and an abiding sense that although he was better than no one, no one was better than him. Throughout the West Indies, strong and loving grandmothers taught these fundamentals of good life and living. These bedrock values and beliefs were Worrell's compass in his life, cricket and leadership. His gentle, loving, and caring wife later buttressed these values in him.

Frank Worrell's first major brush with the authority of the West Indies Cricket Board of Control (WICBC) came in the run-up to the West Indies tour of India in 1948 – 1949. Since the 1920s the WICBC ruled West Indies cricket; much, much later, the word "control" was dropped from its name. It was the WICBC which secured the grant of "test status" for the West Indies in 1928. From the beginning the WICBC was led by white men from the planter-merchant elite. Indeed, during Worrell's playing years the WICBC had known no other President of the WICBC but a white man from the economically-dominant class with attitudes to match. The roll-call of names from 1928 indicates this: Sir H. B. G. Austin

(Barbados), John Dare (British Guiana), Sir Errol Dos Santos (Trinidad), Fred Grant (Trinidad), and Cecil Manley (Jamaica). They were to be followed by R. K. Nunes (Jamaica), and Tom Pierce (Barbados). The last-named was followed by a brown-skinned Jamaican professional, Allan Rae, the first non-white President of WICBC, and who had opened the batting for the West Indies on their successful tour of England in 1950.

There was absolutely no doubt, that all things being equal, Worrell would have been among the top choices in the West Indies' touring squad of sixteen cricketers for the tour of India. After all, during the series immediately preceding the Indian tour, that is the West Indies versus England series in the West Indies in 1948, Worrell had topped the West Indies' batting with an aggregate of 294 runs in four innings (two not outs) and an average per innings of 147.00 runs. The next prolific batsman was Weekes. In his six innings he aggregated 293 runs at an average of 48.33 runs per innings; he stood at number four in the batting averages with G.A. Carew and Jeffrey Stollmeyer above him.

At the time of the selection for the India tour, Worrell was playing League cricket in England, for Radcliffe, as a professional cricketer, at an annual salary of 500 pounds sterling; he played one day per week. He requested of the WICBC a tour salary of 300 pounds sterling, a most reasonable fee for his services on what was to be a gruelling tour. The WICBC refused even after Worrell compromised by indicating his acceptance of the Board's initial non-salaried offer on the understanding that the salary discussion be continued at a later date.

The story in summary form of the Worrell-WICBC dispute is well put by Kenneth Ramchard (with Yvonne Teelucksingh) in the editorial introduction to Jeffrey Stollmeyer's, *The West Indies in India (1948–1949) – Stollmeyer's Diary* published in 2004, after Stollmeyer's death:

> The sixteen selected for the India tour did not include Frank Worrell. According to Stollmeyer in *Everything Under the Sun* (1983), Worrell was being disciplined; the latest incident having been his turning up late for the first day of the fourth test against England at Sabina. According to the matter-of-fact Walcott, however, the Board and Worrell could not come to terms. Michael Manley in *A History of West Indies Cricket* (1988) says that

the twenty-three year old Worrell was showing himself as a man apart, a pioneer and a leader of the future: 'Worrell asked to be paid a reasonable, though still modest, stipend to go to India. The Board treated this as if it were an act of impertinence and refused to negotiate in any reasonable sense, confident that Worrell would come to heel. Born leader that he was, Worrell would not yield and preferred to miss the tour. In that act he served notice that the Black professionals of the post-war era were no longer prepared to be exploited as had been the custom with the giants of yesteryear like Headley and Constantine. Cricket was their life. It must also be their livelihoods'.

Interestingly, on the eve of the West Indies' tour of England in 1963, it was Frank Worrell's turn to persuade a reluctant Sobers to accept the WICBC's stingy offer to tour; Sobers was at the time playing for South Australia; he also played League Cricket in the English summer. In his autobiography, Sobers tells the story thus:

> The pay I was offered as a professional cricketer to go on the tour and play almost everyday was somewhere around 800 pounds sterling, less than I could make playing league cricket once per week. Although we were also given a small daily allowance and our expenses, there were no man-of-the-match awards as there are now and no other perks to bolster the money. I sought advice from Sir Donald Bradman and Richie Bernard who both told me to accept, as did Frank Worrell who wrote to me expressing strongly the reasons why I should go. He talked about representing my country. Of course he was right and I cabled my acceptance. They certainly had their money's worth out of me on that trip as I played in more matches than anyone else in the 18-strong touring party.

Evidently, Worrell's sense of nationalism and the altered and altering socio-political circumstances of West Indies cricket and society provided the context for his advice to Sobers. The entire context was different to that of 1948 when Worrell challenged the authoritarianism and recalcitrance of the colonially-minded WICBC on the eve of that tour to India. Further, Worrell must have considered that Sobers was likely, very shortly, to be next captain of the West Indies and he did not want Sobers to hamper his own future. It is not that Worrell abandoned the principle of the necessity and desirability of adequate payment for a professional cricketer's services, but as always the "context", and not only the "text", is of significance to wise leaders. This is the conundrum which was to face Clive Lloyd and his team at the time of "the Kerry Packer Revolution" in the late 1970s; it is the similar bundle of matrices which more recently confronted Chris Gayle and others in their disagreements with the Board.

Worrell's grasp of the understanding of "context" and "text", history and the future, tactics and strategy, adaptability and constancy, setbacks and advances, the transient and the durable, theory and practice, was to mark his endeavours in life, batting, bowling, and leadership. Examples abound including his adaptability on different types of wickets and weather; the alteration of his bowling styles in an admixture of spin and medium-pace; the switching to left-arm bowling after his right arm was broken as a youngster; his steadfastness to the 'cricket code' and his challenge to it at critical moments; his flexibility and underlying astuteness as player and leader; his understanding of men whom he led which engendered affection, love, discipline, and high quality performance.

The WICBC's failure and/or refusal to appoint Worrell as captain of the West Indies team from at least 1957 onwards was a blatant case of race and class discrimination. To be sure Worrell had had a few disciplinary run-ins, real or contrived, with the authoritarian colonial-minded Board but they were inconsequential. In any event, Worrell's challenges to the Board's unreasonableness and the injustices it meted out to black cricketers under its suzerainty marked him out as a leader. His performance as an all-round cricketer at all levels, including at test cricket against Australia, England and India were magnificent. His knowledge of the game was legendary; his experiences wide and deep; his temperament exemplary for any kind of leadership; his general education of the highest quality; his personal traits of honesty, integrity, and discipline shone through his life and work; his profound West Indianess, nationalism, belief in himself and the West Indian people; and a sense of personal and collective self-mastery, completed the bundle of splendid qualities he brought to the table of life and leadership.

The Caribbean's foremost intellectual of the 20th century and revolutionary activist C. L. R. James, led a focused campaign as editor and nationalist in 1960 from the pages of The Nation, the organ of the People's National Movement of Trinidad and Tobago, of which political party he was General Secretary, for Worrell to be made captain of the West Indies team for the West Indies' tour of Australia scheduled for December 1960 into early 1961. Remember this: No black man had ever captained the West Indies in a test series; only the great George Headley had led the team in a one-off match in 1948.

James' unanswerable case on behalf of Worrell is well-known; he recounted it in his classic *Beyond a Boundary* (1963), and other penetrating writings on cricket and leadership. It was plain madness, extraordinary social and racist arrogance, for the WICBC to have selected an unmeritorious Denis Atkinson of Barbados to captain the West Indies in the first, fourth and fifth tests when the Australians visited us in 1954-1955. On the West Indies team there were men like Worrell, Weekes and Walcott. Amazingly, Atkinson was also selected to lead the West Indies in their tour of New Zealand in 1955-1956. Further, it was an insult to have asked Worrell, Weekes and Walcott to be captained by John Goddard in the West Indies' tour of England in 1957. It was even more insulting and incomprehensible to have a green-horn to test cricket, the Jamaican wicketkeeper and Cambridge Blue, the caucasian F. C. M "Gerry" Alexander to captain the West Indies in Pakistan's tour of the West Indies in 1957-1958 and the West Indies' tour of India in 1958-1959, both of which Worrell missed because of his academic studies at Manchester. Alexander's reappointment as the captain of the West Indies team for the English tour of the Caribbean in 1959-1960 was an unspeakable act of folly in all the circumstances. In that team was Worrell, the accomplished cricketing artist and leader, five years older than Alexander, and the only survivor from the pre-1950 era until Walcott joined the side for the fourth and fifth tests of that 1959-1960 series. On the team, too, were men like Sobers and Kanhai, both more experienced, talented, and wiser in the world of cricket and people than Alexander.

Alexander's elevation to the captaincy of West Indies' cricket was an outrage, the last defiant act of the 'ancien regime' to stem the rising and irreversible tide of West Indian nationalism, mass democratic politics and self-government. Some thirty years previously, James had made the intellectually compelling and politically unanswerable case for West Indian self-government. In 1960, he was at battle again, at the forefront, for a veritable "self-government" at the pinnacle of West Indian cricket, on and off the field. Always the game of cricket was "beyond the boundary". Worrell's time had come. The times they were "a-changing" to use Bob Dylan's memorable line a few years later. Interestingly, the WICBC yielded to popular pressure by appointing Worrell as captain for the 1960-1961 tour of Australia nine-months before its start and in the month of March, 1960, when Alexander was still leading the West Indies against England.

Change was certainly gaining momentum: In 1957, Ghana became independent under the leadership of the African nationalist leader, Kwame Nkrumah; the anti-colonialist and decolonisation movement was spreading rapidly in Africa and Asia; in Latin America, Fidel Castro and his revolutionary July 26th movement had come to power in Cuba and anti-imperialism was on the rise; the Vietnam War involving the Americans against the Vietnamese was in its early stirrings; the civil rights movement in the USA led by Martin Luther King was moving apace; *The Wretched of the Earth* authored by the Martinican-Algerian revolutionary, Franz Fanon, was published in 1960; the West Indian Federation was seeking to find its way amidst heightened nationalist stirrings in most West Indian territories, including Jamaica and Trinidad; popular music and culture were threatening the old order; at the University of the West Indies, intellectuals were descending from "the ivory tower" to address popular concerns in the political economy and society; and the people's democratic struggles were creating new or additional spaces for the enlargement of real freedoms or at least the contestation of social battles on issues of justice, democracy, liberty, and self-government.

Leaders often make their mark after experiencing what may be termed "wilderness years"; wilderness experience ensures that the leader is beaten on the anvil of experience and forged in the cauldron of struggle. The Old Testament is replete with this truism: Moses, Joshua, and the prophet-builder Nehemiah. In other epochs the same story has been, and can be, told: Winston Churchill chosen as the war drums rolled in Europe: Norman Washington Manley in Jamaica as Premier in the 1950s; and Errol Barrow's ascent to high office in Barbados in 1961 they all endured "wilderness years". So, too, Frank Worrell. He had come for this specific time. And as Issachar, one of the leaders of the twelve tribes of Israel, informed us simply and pointedly in the Book of Chronicles: The leader must know and reflect the times!

In a brilliant essay written by C. L. R. James entitled "Sir Frank Worrell" and published in 1970 in John Arlott's *Cricket: The Great Captains*, the following is stated:

> The twentieth century has seen three captains who have expressed a certain stage of cricket and of society. Without some grasp of what they represent, cricket is just a lot of men hitting a ball and running about in flannels. These three men are Pelham Warner, Don Bradman and Frank Worrell.

> ...(After the Bradman era) the systematic refusal to take risks, and to concentrate on what could be reasonably safe dominated cricket for years and, what was worse, did not decline but expanded.

> The man who broke this, and made it clear that the game could and should return to what it had been, was Frank Worrell as captain of the West Indies Test team. It is not too much to say that in the world at large, today and in recent years, we have seen a massive instinctual rejection by people everywhere of the kind of sytematised social organisation which began with the organisation of the economy by J. M. Keynes. This I know is somewhat difficult to accept in regard to a game like cricket, but I cannot think of it otherwise and that is the significance of Frank Worrell as a cricket captain.

This is a large claim but the evidence suggests that James is correct in his assessment. Indeed, one reflective commentator on this matter, the celebrated Caribbean historian Woodville Marshall buttressed the Jamesian analysis in an incisive essay entitled "The Worrell–Sobers Revolution" published in 1994 in Hilary Beckles' edited volume, *An Area of Conquest: Popular Democracy and West Indies Cricket Supremacy.* Marshall identifies three indicators of "the Worrell – Sobers Revolution": the team's success when compared with that of its predecessors; the self-confidence and resilience of the team; and the impact at home and abroad of the team's performance. Marshall persuasively argues that this revolution was effected through four combined factors: captaincy on merit; full recognition for professional cricketers; the adoption of a "professional approach" to the game; and the conscious building of team unity. Of all four elements, Marshall insists: "Captaincy on merit is the key issue". Worrell ensured that his revolution would continue by emphatically building "an axis" with Sobers from 1960-1961 to 1963 inclusive as captain and then as Manager for the 1965 Australian tour of the West Indies. Rohan Kanhai, Clive Lloyd, Vivian Richards, and to some extent, Ritchie Richardson, built and consolidated the West Indies team on the basis of the foundations of this "revolutionary axis".

In *Whispering Death: The Life and Times of Michael Holding*, published in 1993, Holding provides a core reason for the dominance of the world cricket by Clive Lloyd's West Indies as "believing in ourselves". An extension of this self-belief is what the Mexican Nobel Laureate for Literature, Octavio Paz, in *The Labyrinth of Solitude*, called virtue of self-mastery. This sense of self-mastery is what pervaded Worrell's praxis as cricketer, captain, West Indian, and global personality. Self-mastery is at the centre of leadership in any field of human endeavour. It is the antithesis of "learned helplessness", pessimism, excessive caution, ill-discipline, lack of clarity in thought and action, and a pervasive absence of self-worth as an individual, community, and nation.

In an essay entitled "Sir Frank Worrell: The Man Whose Leadership Made History" published in *The Cricketer*, May 5, 1967, (and reprinted in a C L R James collection titled *Cricket* (1987), James wrote aptly:

> He (Worrell) had shown the West Indian mastery of what Western civilisation had to teach. His wide experience, reputation, his audacity of perspective and the years which seemed to stretch before him fitted him to be one of those destined to help the West Indies to make their own West Indian way.

Amazingly, Worrell, a man of reserve, who did not pander to an audience for cheap popularity, emerged as an authentic national hero to the West Indian people in 1960-1961. His status was cemented by performance and the popular imagination's instinctive response to his quest for what James called "the cohesion and self-realisation of the West Indian people". He did what was right by his people without fuss and fanfare; and this fitted him for the exercise of leadership and popular acclaim.

In 1963, the Lord Mayor of London was to remark that the West Indies touring team to England led by Worrell that year represented: "A gale of change (which) has blown through the hallowed halls of cricket". On this accomplishment by Worrell and his men, James was to comment:

> This was no casual achievement. Behind the singular grace and inherent dignity of his manner, Frank Worrell was a man of very strong character. He had himself confessed his strange inability to feel at ease in the society of Barbados. His relations with the West Indies Board of Control earned him the title of a 'cricket Bolshevik'. What is by now obvious is that he was possessed of an almost unbridled passion for social equality. It was the men on his side who had no social status whatever for whose interest and welfare he was always primarily concerned. They repaid him with an equally fanatical devotion.

Leadership, C. L. R James, and Worrell

In *The Decline and Fall of the Roman Empire*, Edward Gibbon averred that leadership is "a heart to resolve, a head to contrive, and a hand to execute". That is a splendid, and even witty, snapshot but it is an incomplete guide to leadership. There is a huge scholastic outpouring on this subject ranging from Niccolo Machiavelli's *The Prince*, through to the discourses by Max Weber and others on charismatic leadership, to Richard Neudstat's advisory to President John Kennedy in the influential book, *Presidential Power*, to the almost theological offerings, including a check-list of leadership qualities, by John Maxwell in his several modern texts on leadership and its functioning, including *The 21 Indispensable Qualities of a Leader*.

A review of the literature on leadership would be exhausting and not necessary for our purposes here. So, I shall make only two points of relevance at the outset and provide, accordingly, brief explanations: One relating to context; the other to leadership application. First, I reiterate that every leadership arises and is sustained by, and within, a particular sociological, political, and formal institutional context. Often the rational-legal or formal institutional apparatuses of, and surrounding, leadership is emphasised without due regard to the sociological, political, and, even historical, underpinnings. This is an error. Obviously, the constitutional and legal framework of, and for, leadership is necessary to any understanding of the exercise of leadership, but it is insufficient. The pre-occupation of traditional political science of the descriptive, formal-legal school has given way to more profoundly sociological, even anthropological, systemic, and non-formal modes of analysis.

The second substantial point on leadership, to which I advert, relates to its application to enhance effectiveness in delivery of the desired outcomes or outputs. I have read many expositions on this subject but perhaps the most incisive has come from C. L. R. James in his celebrated book, *Beyond a Boundary*. James was writing about the leadership of Frank Worrell, the West Indies Cricket Captain, on the West Indies Tour of Australia in 1960-1961. Please remember that the West Indies Touring Team consisted of a disparate group of talented individuals of known quality, some older players of declining cricketing prowess, and some relative unknowns, with promise. Worrell had to facilitate their moulding into a winning unit. Permit me to quote C. L. R. James at length on the leadership question, and please weigh his sparse language carefully:

> As everyone knows, the tour began badly. But, said Worrell, he lectured a few only of his men on taking courses to bring their general knowledge of the appurtenances of life up to the standard expected from so prominent a personage as a Test cricketer; on cricket he lectured nobody.

> 'If something was wrong I told them what was right and left it to them', (Worrell said).

> These words will always ring in my ears. They are something new, not only in West Indies cricket but in West Indies life. West Indians can often tell you what is wrong and some even what will make it right, but they don't leave it to you. Worrell did. It is the ultimate expression of a most finished personality, who knows his business, theory and practice, and knows modern men.

...The West Indies team in Australia, on the field and off, was playing above what it knew of itself. If anything went wrong it knew that it would be instantly told, in unhesitating and precise language, how to repair it, and that the captain's certainty and confidence extended to his belief that what he wanted would be done. He did not instill into but drew out of his players. What they discovered must have been a revelation to a few more than to the players themselves.

From all this I learn that a leader, including a cricketing or political leader, must know intimately the resources which he possesses at hand; he/she must assess properly the strengths and weaknesses, possibilities and limitations of the persons (and institutions) who are being led; he/she must seek to lift the general knowledge of those whom he/she is leading so as to enable them to make wise decisions in their day-to-day work; the leader must have confidence in the capacity of those who are being led to do the right thing, to do their best; the leader must have goals for the collective to achieve within which frame each individual has his/her responsibilities; the leader must guide and point the way forward; the leader must work actively at his/her tasks and not merely talk; the leader must not be overly cautious and always play it safe; he/she must not be afraid of making errors but must not be a friend of recklessness; he/she must learn from his/her errors and those of others. Above all, I learn from C. L. R. James on this subject that inspiring persons whom you are leading is important but far more important and more challenging, is to draw out of them that which is good and noble in them; even to draw out goodness and nobility from them which they do not as yet know that they possess. Leadership thus is an art (not a science); it is clearly a talent which some people have and others do not.

In cricket, as in politics, leadership is an intellectual, creative, and people-centred activity. Without a compelling narrative about our condition and the way forward for the people, the leader would not only mark time, but regress into a host of "ad hoc" interventions of little or no positive consequence. Inertia would inevitably set in; defensiveness and backwardness would prevail. Trivia and side-shows would preoccupy the leader's agenda. A debilitating malaise of "learned helplessness" would set in. The administration of things would be reduced to the routinisation of stasis without any developmental thrust; and the very routinisation process itself would become mired in lethargy, petty corruption, and even mere malicious compliance. The regime would be unable to rule in the old way but would be at sea since it knows no other way but the old way which is itself untenable. In short measure, an internal crisis may evolve or develop. The crisis generally, and in leadership, emerges when the principals are innocent of the extent of the challenging, dangerous or unacceptable condition and has no clear idea or frame of reference for the way forward out of the crisis.

The "compelling narrative" of the political leadership in these Caribbean states ought to be comprised of: a clearly-articulated people-centred vision of sustainable development; a political philosophy of social democracy applied to the national Caribbean conditions; a socio-cultural framework of the legitimacy of our Caribbean civilisation and its trajectory for further advancement and ennoblement; an economic framework in quest of building a modern, many-sided competitive post-colonial economy which is at once national, regional and global; a package of relevant public policies and practical programmes derived therefrom for overall socio-economic development, enhanced good governance and citizen security; a practical commitment to deepening regional integration; a foreign policy which focuses on international solidarity for the people's benefit but lodged within the framework of the principled ideals of the charter of the United Nations; and an effective system of public management (administration) to implement this overarching yet specific, "compelling narrative".

Such a leadership in politics would provide a political context which would impact positively on cricket, its leadership, and administration.

In 1926, after the end of his first-class cricketing career (1893-1920), one of the sport's distinguished captains, the Australian, M.A. Noble, wrote in his book *The Game's the Thing* about captaincy and leadership as follows:

> Many qualifications are necessary adequately to equip the man selected as captain, and he may learn just so much as his mentality will allow. There is, however, one attribute that cannot be acquired: it is a gift of the gods, and may be summed up in the phrase 'personal equation'. When he possesses that most valuable

trait, it goes without saying that the men under his command have great personal respect for him and faith in his judgment. He becomes a tower of strength, a rock to lean upon in adversity. He inspires such confidence that they will work hard, keep 'on their toes', and combine to give of their best no matter how long the way or how tired they are. His keenness and enthusiasm are infectious, and his men respond readily and without effort. It is this dominant force that is of such tremendous value to the side. Emerson once said: 'There is no company of men so great as one man.' In a cricket sense that is particularly true. The great leader is the embodiment of all the hopes, virtue, courage and ability possessed by ten men under his command. If he is not, he is but the shadow and lacks the substance of captaincy. He will not last.

On the valued measures of James and Noble, there has been no more accomplished leader than Worrell in West Indies cricket, by far. I am always taken aback when commentators select the notional "best combined West Indies team" and exclude Frank Worrell. He is arguably the second best all-round cricketer, after Sobers, whom the West Indies have produced and he is the best captain, ever. If one doubts the significance of leadership, note carefully again the words of Noble:

> Captaincy has much greater influence on the fate of a match than is often realised. The side possessing a capable leader has a great advantage. No two men are alike. The only times captains are reduced to the same level is in the spinning of the coin. One may have a run of luck, but he can never have a run of character, and even the toss will even itself up in the long run.

I feel sure, for example, without Worrell at the helm, the West Indies would have lost "the tied test" at Brisbane in December 1960 and the fourth test of that series against Australia at Adelaide in February 1961, which was drawn. Without Worrell's leadership, too, the West Indies most assuredly would have lost, rather than drawn, the second test against England at Lord's in June 1963. In each case, his extraordinary leadership held the team together on occasions of extreme challenges and drew the best out of his men, even that which they did not know they possessed.

In the case of the "Tied Test" at Brisbane, Worrell's opponent as captain, Richie Benaud wrote as follows in his book *On Reflection* (1984):

When things threatened to get out of hand, Frank (Worrell) was there with his calm air of authority, his smile, and the husky laugh which was instantly recognisable at a distance by anyone who had played with or against him. I saw all this at first hand in the Tied Test on the final afternoon because I had to bat for much of the time with Alan Davidson in what was akin to a limited-overs situation. We knew roughly how many overs we would receive even off Wes Hall's longest, longest run, and how many runs were needed, and we made our plans accordingly.

Frank (Worrell) made his plans which involved the new ball, taken at 200 runs in those days, and the careful use of Wes Hall and Garry Sobers mixed in with Ramaddin and Valentine. You could tell the West Indies were under pressure by some of their throwing in the field and from the tension in the centre. You could also tell that there was little likelihood of them crumbling under pressure because of one incident. When Joe Solomon threw down the stumps to run out Davidson whilst Sobers was bowling, Alexander was up over the stumps for the throw – not on the run but actually over the stumps – and there were two men backing up.

After that dismissal Worrell kept telling his men to concentrate and relax. It is not all that easy to do both at the same moment, but the idea was right. 'Relax fellas, relax' came the call time after time. When Wes Hall made a nonsense of catching Wally Grout at square-leg — square-leg mind you next to the umpire — off his own bowling, knocking over Rohan Kanhai at the same time, Frank never for one instant allowed annoyance to show through. Instead, he walked over to Hall, put his arm around his shoulders and told him...to relax. Talking with Wes (Hall) a few years after the event, he told me this was one of the worse moments of his life. He thought he had thrown away the Test match for his country and it was Worrell's calming influence which again got him back on the rails.

The comprehensive and overwhelming clean-sweep, five-to-nil victory in the series against India in the West Indies in 1962 was due to a significant degree to Worrell's leadership and the moulding of a professional, unified outfit in the aftermath of the epic series against Australia in Australia in 1960–1961. In two tests India went down to innings defeats; in two other tests India lost by seven and ten wickets respectively; and in the fifth test India lost by 123 runs. To be sure, the batting of Worrell, Kanhai and Sobers, and the bowling of Hall, Gibbs, Sobers (and Lester King in the final test) were outstanding but Worrell's marshalling of the troops was a marvel to behold.

In the West Indies' tour of England in 1963, Worrell's leadership made a huge difference in the West Indies' overwhelming three-to-one victory margin in the five-test series: The first test win was by a margin of 10 wickets; the fourth test by a victory of 221 runs (after a loss to England by 217 runs in the third test); and the fifth test by a victory margin of eight wickets. And in the drawn second test at Lord's, Worrell's leadership was masterful down to the wire on the final day. It was as though this master could do no wrong; the grip on his team was almost metaphysical; and the bonding was of a caring and loving nature. It appeared magical, but it was real! The lordly Ted Dexter, the English captain, was simply no match for Worrell.

Leadership demands strategic, visionary thinking but also requires attention to details and "getting the small things right". Leading young men in world sport is particularly problematic: How to regulate or control their nocturnal excursions? Are late night curfews to be imposed, and if so, what, when and how? What about their consumption of alcohol, its type and quantities? Are they to be permitted to engage in any activity which may inhibit or undermine their performance at the game?

Worrell was able to achieve with his players a balanced admixture of freedom, personal choice, individual responsibility and collective obligation which satisfied the men-under-his-command, individually, and the requisites of the team as a whole. He, however, prohibited the playing of cards, at least excessively, since he held the view that it adversely affected the cricketer's eye-body coordination and thus his performance on the field. His experience and study of this phenomenon had led him to this conclusion. Both Walcott and Sobers commented on this Worrell stricture in their autobiographies.

Twenty years ago, in March 1992, in an article authored by me entitled "Leadership in Cricket: Windwards and the West Indies" (published in *The News Cricket Souvenir*, March 21, 1992) I made the following summary assessment of Worrell's leadership:

> I agree with the comment made by the former Australian cricket captain, Richie Benaud, during Vivian Richards' incumbency, that the West Indies have had two great captains: Frank Worrell and Clive Lloyd. Their claim to greatness lies not simply in their technical mastery of the game of cricket, their astuteness on the field of play, their tactical flexibility, their strategic formulations, their probing analysis of the game generally and the state of play of particular matches, their instinctive grasp of what to do when and how, their own vital contributions with bat or ball, and their general management of the team.

> To be sure, all these factors helped to stamp Worrell's and Lloyd's leadership with the mark of greatness. But they were not enough. Indeed, some cricket captains, for example Garfield Sobers and Rohan Kanhai, possessed much of the aforementioned attributes, yet they were unable to achieve greatness as captains. The greatness of Worrell's and Lloyd's leadership rested on something more profound: their capacity to have taken a group of talented individuals and moulded them into an organic whole in such a way that their individual strengths and weaknesses were diffused into the whole with the result that the whole became more than a summation of the individual parts.

> It is from this perspective that one can easily unravel the ungenerous tautology of the uninformed critics who prattle that Worrell and Lloyd were great only because they had great teams. It is often forgotten that both Worrell and Lloyd fashioned their highly successful teams only after having turned setbacks into advances: in Worrell's case it was a seven-wicket thrashing by

Australia at Melbourne in the second test in the 1960-61 series; in Lloyd's, it was the humiliation of the 1975-76 debacle in Australia.

This organic conception of leadership stands in stark contrast to the mechanistic view. The latter extols the individual qua individual; the former comes to terms with the centrality of "wholeness" within which the creativity and flair of the individual have abundant space for expression and fulfillment. In the process, Worrell and Lloyd organically transformed the talented individual into a "social" or "collective" individual with wholesome and indivisible connections to the body corporate known as the team and with the West Indian community at home and in the diaspora.

Worrell's Paradigm on Leadership and Cricket in the Era of Globalisation

What, therefore, in summary, can we learn from Worrell's life, cricket and leadership — the Worrell paradigm — to assist us in successfully confronting the challenges which beset. West Indian cricket, culture, society, and political economy?

Thomas Kuhn, global thinker and scientist, in *The Structure of Scientific Revolutions* (1962) defines "a paradigm" as that:

Constellation of values, beliefs, perceptions of empirical reality, which, together with a body of theory based upon the foregoing, is used by a group of scientists, and by applying a distinctive methodology, to interpret the nature of some aspect of the universe which we inhabit.

Surely, by this definition, there is as we have shown extensively, a "Worrell paradigm" to assist us in the interpretation of much confusing reality around us, particularly in the field of cricket and society.

99

I start with a query concerning a substantial part of the reality around us in cricket posed by Boria Majumdar in his book *An Illustrated History of Indian Cricket,* published in 2007:

> In the Victorian era, cricket was an Anglo-Saxon political tool to civilise the world. Today is an Eastern economic imperialism rooted in cricket about to commence?

I ask: What are the implications of all this for cricket, the global political economy, and the Caribbean's place in it?

Modern globalism in its advanced form has gripped human civilisation in an all pervasive manner consequent upon the collapse of centrally-planned economies, the Cold War, and the international political architecture of the so-called "socialist bloc". The extraordinary spread of finance capital, the rise of casino capitalism divorced from the real production of goods and services, the emergence of a fully-charged "turbo-capitalism" especially in Brazil, Russia, India and China ("the BRIC" countries), the decline of the unipolar world of American dominance and an accompanying multi-polarity in the world's political economy, the technological revolutions in information processes and biotechnology, have all combined to effect phenomenal shifts in wealth, power, and influence globally.

Of the BRICS and other emerging economies, including South Africa, India is the cricketing nation of rising wealth, power and influence. India's population stands at 1.2 billion, and rising fast; half of them are under 25 years old. India's economy has been growing in recent years at rates between four and ten percent annually. India's cricket audience is estimated at over 500 million people, more than the combined cricket-loving constituencies of the other major cricketing nations of Australia, England, Bangladesh, New Zealand, Pakistan, South Africa, Sri Lanka, the West Indies, and Zimbabwe.

India is a nation of huge diversities and contradictions. Billionaires and multi-millionaires drawn from the list of the richest 100 individuals in the world, on the one hand, and extreme poverty on the other – forty percent of its children are under-nourished and live in indigence; a world-class information industry but a limited spread of the internet, water and electricity; an extraordinary growth of popular television, cinema and radio, but massive rural under-development; extremes of corruption and religious piety; a modernising economic system and unreformed administrative apparatus; a nation united under one flag but experiencing profound social fissures based on differences lodged in religion, ethnicity, caste, geography, wealth, and access to opportunities. Cutting across all these differences in this magnificent, inspiring country, is an extraordinary passion and love for cricket. The British Raj, its accomplices, and nationalist successors have done a fantastic job of making cricket "the second religion" for practically every Indian.

The opportunities arising from cricket to be exploited by the market are simply phenomenal. This growth area has empowered the Board of Control for Cricket in India (BCCI) nationally and internationally in cricket; has caused umbilical connections to be strengthened and solidified between business, cricket administrators, cricketers, popular culture, and politicians; has caused new formats such as Twenty-Twenty Cricket to be enthroned to the detriment of traditional cricket in test matches and one-day internationals; and has placed the lucrative Indian Premier League (IPL) on a collision course with the regulatory world body of cricket, the International Cricket Council (ICC). The market and tradition are at war over the current trajectory and future condition of cricket. In the process, communities and nations are in danger of being sacrificed on the altar of a rampaging modern capitalism; individual cricketers, especially "the super-stars", are having their ties to their respective nations loosened as they become global property for sale to the highest bidder. Top class cricketers now have agents, lawyers, accountants, and financial managers in touch with each other constantly by way of the modern gadgets of the cell-phone and the lap-top. Reassessments are evidently in order on notions of nation, community, individualism, authority, the governance of cricket, and the role of the market. These are subjects which engender an abundance of emotion but we must approach them dispassionately. The guiding principles are to seek truth from facts; let the real world validate the truth; and act in the interests of the people as a whole. It certainly is not a time for hand-wringing abstractions, vanities, and head-in-the-sand approaches. In all this we must never lose sight, too, of certain basic truisms that cricket is a team sport, played for enjoyment and entertainment, but pregnant with real meaning and possibilities for the further ennoblement of our West Indian people within, and beyond, the boundary. In short, we must never forget that it is a core cultural feature of our Caribbean civilisation, whilst acknowledging the benefits to be derived for it from the market without it being commodified lock, stock and barrel.

The pristine notion of the nation-state, and its political adornment, sovereignty, arose in the aftermath of the Thirty Years War in Europe and was codified in the Treaty of Westphalia in 1648. The community of oneness of a people, and the territorial boundaries within which it is structured, predated the nation-state itself, and continues to exist tenaciously and thrive even in a context where the globalisation of the economy, culture, technology, governance, and instruments of war has eroded the pristine, self-contained nature of the nation-state. A national community continues to resonate because peoples of common origin, language and cultural oneness do feel that they possess an identity which differentiates them from others. Further, a living civilisation is defined, in part, by the permanence of its people in a specific geographic landscape and seascape. To be sure, this national community becomes penetrated, and even compromised or altered, on account of the fact that its peoples are influenced and shaped by the invasive processes of regionalism and globalisation.

Thus, professional cricketers observe that commercial enterprises, bankers, and other individual professionals engage in cross-border trading of their goods and services and ask why they cannot do the same, unfettered by cricket authorities nationally, regionally, or internationally. The answer is that the professional cricketer is perfectly at liberty to do so, but the other non-sporting professionals do not ever compete under the rubric of a national or regional umbrella. So, if a professional cricketer considers that being part of a national or regional outfit adds prestige and value to his personal brand, which additional value or prestige he craves, he must be prepared to subject himself to the authority and requisites of national or regional authority or structure which manages and/or superintends the cricket.

But does this mean that the national or regional cricketing authority has unlimited jurisdiction over the professional cricketer and his capacity or ability to sell his professional services? Clearly not! The law of the land prohibits unreasonable restraint of trade; it respects contracts duly entered upon; and it accords reasonable protection to a player's "intellectual property" rights, and those of the team.

Complicating this business is the fact that a cricketing authority such as the West Indies Cricket Board (WICB) does not own the good or service which is being produced by the cricketers. It is a public good or service produced by cricketers under the organizational aegis and authority of the WICB but in a communal partnership with the State and other non-State actors. Cricket is, and has always been, a collective enterprise for, and of, West Indian people, even when managed by a "private" entity. All this makes the delivery of the cricketing service unique and special in the West Indies.

The resolution of the tensions between the individual cricketer in pursuit of his personal financial rewards and the community which demands that its best players be on their West Indies team, resides in the rejection of the notion of the individual qua individual, the apotheosis of an atomized individual, and the embrace of the idea of the social individual whereby the individual cricketer establishes and sustains an organic relationship with the community. The community and its supportive national/regional cricket institutions are obliged, among other things, to accord proper compensation and other rewards or incentives as part of the material basis for sustaining the organic nexus between community, team, and individual player.

This era is not the first in which the issue of a reasonable payment for cricketer's services, has arisen. This has been the case with Worrell, Sobers, Hall, and others, at different periods in our history. But these were individual, not systemic challenges, which were resolved in one way or another without too much hiccup. The so-called "Kerry Packer Revolution", with enhanced benefits for players; innovations in cricket gear, presentation, and rules; and parallel "national" teams of the most gifted cricketers in his "World Series" competition, was resolved in favour of the entrepreneur (Kerry Packer) after the Australian Cricket Board conceded to Packer the television rights for Australian cricket which he had originally sought.

The "Kerry Packer Revolution" strengthened rather than weakened the game of cricket for the players and public alike. The old-fashioned aristocratic personages in the ICC and the outmoded types who managed cricket authorities across the test-playing countries, including the planter-merchant elements in the West Indies, suffered a loss of authority and prestige. But progressive modern capitalism, as represented by an entrepreneurial Packer, is always likely to win out against a nostalgic plantation-mercantile capitalism with all its historical baggage. In that conflict the Law Courts in England reaffirmed a bundle of basic rights of professional cricketers and turned askance against the ICC quest to restrain trade. The upshot is that "the old order" accommodated itself to "the new" amidst organisational reforms, concessions to the players, and some altered modes of cricket.

In 2006–2008, the antics of the Stanford Financial Empire, headquartered in Antigua, momentarily threatened to shake-up West Indian and world cricket. This, however, was brought crashing with the arrest of its owner in 2009. Historically, the Allen Stanford Twenty-Twenty Cricket would be seen as a sideshow if only because it was episodic buccaneering, which nevertheless had seduced "the lords" of English cricket, the ICC, the WICB, players from England and the West Indies, and "the legends" from the West Indies. With memorable exceptions, the West Indian community, and others, dropped their guard to the Stanford glitz and dazzle.

The current challenge by the IPL, and the BCCI, to international cricket as hitherto organised is unprecedented. Its closest parallel, "the Kerry Packer Revolution" was comparatively limited in its scope, power, and clout. In any event the Packer "World Series" fielded "national sides" albeit through a private entrepreneur. The IPL consists of Indian-based franchises in the form of clubs or teams financed by many individual conglomerates in a period of globalisation. Fundamentally, the Packer challenge was peculiarly Australian with a global knock-on effect. The IPL-BCCI venture is ambitiously and intentionally global in its reach for players, and television audience, for Twenty-Twenty games, not unofficial "test matches", but resting comfortably and lucratively on a burgeoning India and a base of one-half of a billion persons at home. The size of this base and the billions of dollars (American dollars) involved, mark it as very different from the Packer enterprises, which lasted for only two or so years.

Karl Marx once observed that all facts and personages of great importance in world history occur, as it were twice: the first time as tragedy, the second as farce. But the threat to the established global cricket order has nothing farcical about it; it has the potential for tragedy in a way which the Packer adventure never had. A keen observer of this unfolding drama is Gideon Haigh, an Australian journalist, who has compiled 71 of his penetrating essays on cricket in a book entitled *Sphere of Influence: Writing on Cricket and its Discontents* published in 2011. In an introductory essay he gets to one of his central themes quickly:

> Cricket is a micro-worrier. Its Laws are voluminous, its codes of conduct and definitions of fair play constantly expanding, its systems of adjudication neurotic in their sophistication. Yet the truly big issues, like its governance structure and global economy, there is a kind of studied indifference. The International Cricket Council? Beyond redemption. The Board of Control for Cricket in India? Beyond restriction. The players? Too greedy. The media? Too cynical. Can we just watch, please? We'll be good, really we will – just don't let them take our lovely game away.

> What constitutes cricket's welfare, meanwhile, is seldom addressed in other than banal terms. Cricket must grow. Cricket must change with the times. Cricket must expand its audience.

Is the West Indian Cricket Board (WICB) fully engaged strategically to influence change, for the better, globally and to guide or manage that change regionally in the people's interest? Is the WICB so preoccupied with extinguishing fires as they arise, some lit by itself, and thus has little time left for cricket's overall development? Is the WICB, including its principal functionaries, too isolated from the players, former players, the public, and the West Indian governments to perform its developmental and managerial roles efficaciously? Is the WICB structured in a manner appropriate to deliver its outputs effectively? These are the sort of queries that a probing Worrell would have raised!

The WICB is one of the ten full (test playing) members of the ICC: Australia, England, India, New Zealand, Pakistan, South Africa, Sri Lanka, West Indies, Bangladesh and Zimbabwe. The ICC also has 34 associate and 60 affiliate members. But that is the formal apparatus. As Haigh points out:

> In reality, such a large proportion of the game's commercial activity and fans are located in India that nothing happens without the say-so of the mahouts aboard the thirty-one-member elephant that is the BCCI, whose annual revenues for 2010-2011 were set to exceed US $400 million. And modern cricket's lucrative instability stems from nowhere but the BCCI's creation of supranational 20-20 attractions beyond the jurisdiction of the ICC, offering rewards by comparison with which those in the established international game pale.

Gideon Haigh details and analyses it all brilliantly. Thus, I draw heavily on his reportage and insights on the 20-20 rave, the BCCI and its Indian Premier League (IPL). He is persuasive about the deleterious impact of it all on test cricket and even on one-day international cricket.

It is ironic that at first Indian cricket administrators thought that one-day cricket was, in the words of BCCI's Chairman of Selectors Rag Singh Dungapur in 1983, "artificial" and "irrelevant". That was before the 1983 World Cup when India were 66-to-one outsiders. These "outsiders", of course, won the tournament, converted India to a diet of one-day games. Their initial aversion to "Twenty-Twenty" cricket was similar. For example, in 2006, BCCI President Pawar argued that Twenty-Twenty cricket "dilutes the importance of international cricket" at the time when Allen Stanford was cranking up the first round of his Twenty-Twenty spectacle in Antigua. No doubt some in India, looking ahead, feared the possible loss of television revenue for their games in India. It was reported, too, that at an ICC Executive Board meeting, Niranjan Shah of India was heard to ask derisively: "Twenty-Twenty? Why not ten-ten or five-five or one-one?" By 2008, the IPL was launched with lucrative franchises in tow. The auctioning for international stars at cricket was introduced; splendour, Bollywood and cricketainment were supplied. A money-spinner had emerged grandly on the Indian stage. Television audiences soared; and women became fanatical cricket enthusiasts. Within three years, by 2011, IPL had expanded from sixty to ninety-four matches crowed over 40-odd days.

From the West Indies, players rushed to the IPL. Allen Stanford had whetted their appetites and pointed to lucrative possibilities for their talented services. The IPL was the next port of call. The bulk of the West Indian people, from the sidelines, cheered on the players, both the experienced and inexperienced ones, in the selling of their skills to the highest bidder. After all, there is a market economy which the economically-dominant class has been trumpeting in unfettered and glorious terms, an aggressive "free market" ideology. Why now, the people were asking should the cricketers, who have risen from the proletariat, be persuaded to deny themselves some substantial earnings from "the free market", in their short careers, by appeals to community-spiritedness and nationhood. By and large these appeals have been spearheaded by those who live in relative comfort and security, without sacrifices, most of whom are beneficiaries of the same unfettered god of market capitalism. Further, despite the fact that WICB had undergone change in its structure and personnel from the days of the planter-merchant elite, the people still were finding it difficult to side with the Board in any conflict with the professional cricketers.

At least three queries arise from all this for commentary: First, should the discourse on the quest for the pot of gold by the professional cricketers be distorted by the undoubted hypocrisy of those who worship at "the god of free market" and yet prattle their view of community, nationalism, and patriotism? Relatedly, should we not ask instead what is in the interest of the people and the cricketers as "social", as distinct from "atomized", individuals? And is an excessive diet of Twenty-Twenty cricket good for the game of cricket nationally and globally?

Surely, it must be a matter of time that an unregulated "multi-billion dollar baby" known as the IPL Twenty-Twenty competition, would come to grief. Experience teaches that casino or turbo-charged capitalism will crumble under its internal weight of largely unregulated practices. Excessive money inevitably attracts undesirables; and a crash is likely to come sooner or later. Increasingly, players are treated as commodities, albeit expensive commodities, and are likely to become alienated from themselves and their trade. In time, the public, Indian and international, are likely to tire at the contrivances of Twenty-Twenty cricket, the quality of which is becoming monotonous and boring. Most of the players in the IPL are sub-standard and gimmicks cannot paper over cracks and inferior batting, bowling and fielding. In time, the quality players in Twenty-Twenty who were groomed for traditional test cricket, through various levels, will inevitably leave the stage; those who replace them are likely to be pale imitations since their skills would not have been honed through intelligence, discipline, patience, mental toughness and fitness.

Players are already complaining that the rigours of travel across India, the off-field demands of sponsors, the parties with the "hoi polloi" and low lifes, and the sheer monotony are sapping their energy, will, and dignity. To be sure, the pay is good but the human spirit suffers and rebels even in gilded cages and sumptuous living. The parents across India and the Caribbean who see pots of gold at the end of the surfeit of Twenty-Twenty rainbows for their children, must ponder carefully on the matter.

The evidence is overwhelming, too, that an unrelenting excess of Twenty-Twenty cricket undermines the sport as a sustainable recreational activity of a civilised people. Fast foods are no substitutes for gourmet meals, even though one grabs a bite quickly at Mc Donalds or Kentucky Fried Chicken, occasionally. I find the testimony of an Indian opening batsman of the Kolkata Knight Riders, Aakash Chopra, truthful and persuasive in his book *Beyond the Blues*, published in 2009:

> Not long ago, playing first-class cricket was the only reason for our existence. Everything revolved around making it to the state team, doing well to secure a berth for the next level and eventually playing for your country. You would spend hours trying to hone the skills more likely to see you through in the longer format of the game.... Performing in the shorter format would take you only so far and as far as playing for the country was concerned..... It was your performance in the longer format that counted.

Players now might get swayed by the rewards of an offer in the Twenty 20 format and hence ignore the importance of playing first-class cricket. Lasting five days on the field and performing at your peak not only needs skills but also a different level of mental and physical fitness. To maintain that level, you have to push yourself to the hilt..... One the other hand, Twenty 20 matches last only a few hours, the tournament is scheduled to happen once a year over a period of forty-five days, and though they require a different set of skills and physical and mental attributes, you don't have to push yourself hard for the rest of the year.... I may be sounding like a cynic, but isn't there a potential threat to the way people approach the game?

I've spoken to a lot of people who have played 20-20 Cricket at the highest level and their response is similar – there is a lot of fun but no real cricket pleasure in the format. It's ideal for viewers, but for cricketers it's more like a lottery.... A lot of players involved in the IPL have, at some stage in their career, voiced their dislike for this format but are more than willing to take part in this mega event. No prizes for guessing what draws everyone to this billion-dollar baby of cricket.

It is thus imperative for the ICC and the BCCI to work out a "modus vivendi" to ensure that cricket as a true test of sporting skills survives and, at the same time, fashion an accommodating framework for television and crowd spectacles such as Twenty-Twenty cricket. An appropriate resolution has to be found for the category known as "the freelance cricketer": that gifted player who renounces international cricket so as to be able to sell his services on the international Twenty-Twenty circuit without the obligation of providing the IPL, for example, with a "No Objection Certificate" (the NOC) from his own Board or Authority. Obviously, if no proper regulatory regime is devised, such a player would always be very valuable to the franchises because of his unrestricted availability.

Surely, though, a "freelance player" cannot reasonably be expected "to cherry pick" which matches or tours he plays, for his national team, such as the West Indies, so as to keep in him currency, literally. A professional must appreciate that he cannot have his cake and eat it no matter how popular he may be with his home crowds. Indeed, our people are unlikely to countenance a one foot in, one foot out stance by anyone. They will continue to support a player's right to ply his trade but they will quite properly turn askance against anyone who opportunistically seeks to misuse or abuse the community and nation which have nurtured him thus far. All these considerations demand that the ICC and the BCCI hammer out amicably the challenge of the IPL to the sustainability of test cricket and one-day internationals.

The conundrum at hand was recently addressed by Hilary Beckles in a thoughtful article published in *The Barbados Advocate* (Sunday April 15, 2012) entitled "Cricket, Cash and Country". Beckles faced this issue head-on:

> What is the disturbing reality that resides at the core? The West Indies is the only nation in Test Cricket that currently finds itself unable to place its best team on the field of play. The nation is under-presented. The young and brightest within our sight are not yet the best, and the team on the field is short on depth of experience. There is no doubt, say all the experts at the Oval over the weekend (in the West Indies versus Australia test match), that our defeat was the result of this circumstance. Indeed, I agreed, that the opportunity to defeat India at home and abroad on recent tours was due precisely to this cause. Mighty Australia, I also agreed, would crumble on tour were we to field our best team.

> Here is the problem. West Indians are the only test cricketers in the world who are able to successfully reject their national duty in preference for a bigger personal purse. An Australian official informed me that no Australian player if called to the Test team could refuse national representation and survive with respect in the nation. Prime Minister, the media, the private sector, and civic society would find the choice unacceptable; they would describe it a rejection of citizenship; an abandonment of the nation. The same political circumstance no doubt applies to England, South Africa, New Zealand, and Pakistan. Such a player would be divested of house and happiness in India; and maybe a great deal more.

I understand Hilary Beckles' point of the importance and high value of embracing the nation and representing it at cricket. I am not sure, though, that he is correct in suggesting there is stronger nationalist sentiment among cricketers of other test playing nations than those from the West Indies. For example, I have seen an authoritative report by Gideon Haigh, from the annual survey of Australian first-class players by the Australian Cricketers' Association which found that two-thirds could foresee one of their peers declining a Cricket Australia contract in order to pursue a freelance career, but 98 percent had "never considered" doing so themselves. Further, we ought to recall that in July 2009 that six New Zealand test cricketers (Daniel Vettori, Brendan Mc Cullum, Jacob Oram, Ross Taylor, Jesse Ryder, and Kyle Mills) signed national contracts only after ensuring that they had preserved their right to play IPL. Indeed, Vettori was quoted at the time as uttering the following words: "We realise that if these situations continue to come up, it will be difficult for players to continue to turn down the money. So, we implore the powers that be to find a solution so we don't have to make these decisions every year." Additionally, we must remember that Andrew Symonds, the test player from Australia, perhaps tired of official restraints on his conduct, signed a contract with the Deccan Chargers for six-weeks work in the IPL for US $1.35 million rather than serving under his national colours. Similarly, Andrew Flintoff, England's former captain, admittedly in his declining years, opted for a US $1.55 million fee for one season in the IPL for the Chennai Super Kings rather than holding himself out for the rigours of English test cricket. Did Flintoff prefer the life of "ignoble ease" in the IPL to that of the "strenuous life" under England's colours? I doubt that; the matter is far more complicated.

I assert, however, that I do not consider any current West Indian test player who participates in the IPL as being in any shape or form less patriotic, less nationalist, or more mercenary than his fellow-professional from Australia, England, New Zealand, Pakistan or anywhere else. I do not include India in this since their BCCI fathered and mothered the IPL, so that none of the Indian test players is in any danger of being orphans in their national land. Beckles is nevertheless right in suggesting that the post-Richards generation of West Indian cricketers appear more representative, than hitherto, of "an unfettered economic individualism, a mentality that is consistent with the general policy and practice of the post-IMF supported states". Still, in this context a reminder is in order that a galaxy of cricket nationalists of yesteryear including Viv Richards, Garfield Sobers, Everton Weekes, Curtly Ambrose, Joel Garner, Lance Gibbs, West Hall, Desmond Haynes, Richie Richardson, Andy Roberts and Courtney Walsh signed on as Stanford "Legends", each reportedly for a handsome monthly fee. They were the attractive front for Allen Stanford's Twenty-Twenty and his incursions into West Indies cricket. Were these icons of our cricketing history accomplices in Stanford's public relations gimmicks which masked or hid what the Securities and Exchange Commission called "a fraud of shocking magnitude"? Absolutely not! They knew not what Stanford was up to; they accepted him at face-value for something which they thought rightly or wrongly would give West Indies cricket a boost; in the process they earned an honest fee. How were they to know of Stanford's fraudulent activities? After all, a Caribbean government had caused him to be knighted for his services to its own development and it ought to have had the requisite "due diligence" on him. These issues are not always straightforward and amenable to sweeping polemical judgments.

So, my assessments of the role of our cricketers in the IPL and that of the 'legends' in Stanford's Twenty-Twenty Cricket are more nuanced. In any event, it is part of our cricketing culture to give the man at the crease, the benefit of a reasonable doubt. Across our region, some governments secure reelection because of our people's reliance on this 'cricketing dictum".

Gayle-WICB Saga and the Future

It would be unusual if I were to duck commentary on the related matter of what has gone recently into our history and folklore as the Chris Gayle-WICB Saga. First, let me say that it is my view that Frank Worrell would not have been unsympathetic to Gayle. His intuitive and learned intelligence and his balanced judgment would more than likely have informed him that to the extent that Gayle transgressed with his critical comments on radio about the management and coach of West Indies cricket, his infraction was minimalist. It is likely that he would have seen that the cricketing authority over-reacted and enveloped itself in the hubris of vanity. I feel sure that he would have urged Gale to make an "expression of regret" for the alleged offending comments and would have sought to persuade the WICB to put the matter behind them swiftly, not allow it to fester, and to move forward in concert in the interest of West Indies Cricket and our civilisation.

As the Prime Minister who was assigned the active role of engaging Gayle and the WICB in the resolution discussions under the aegis of the CARICOM Prime Ministerial Sub-Committee on Cricket chaired by Prime Minister Baldwin Spencer of Antigua-Barbuda, I was struck by the profound commitment of all the relevant individuals to West Indies Cricket and nation. Julian Hunte (President of WICB), Ernest Hilaire (Chief Executive Office of WICB), Otis Gibson (Coach of the West Indies Team) and Chris Gayle, all West Indians and patriots and professionals of merit and distinction. Hunte is a self-made businessman, accomplished diplomat and Foreign Minister of St. Lucia who served as the elected President of the General Assembly of the United Nations. Hilaire, also St. Lucian, is a highly educated professional with a post-graduate qualification from Cambridge University and experienced in politics and public administration. Gibson, a former test cricketer from Barbados, a former Wisdem cricketer of the year for his performance in English country cricket, a trained and accredited cricket coach, and former bowling coach of the English test team – experienced and sharply intelligent and articulate. And Gayle, a world class opening batsman from Jamaica, and a former captain of the West Indies test team.

I sensed though that there was a mistrust between the WICB and its principals on the one hand and Gayle on the other which was rooted in cultural issues, poor communication, and less-than cordial inter-personal relations from the past. But what joined them together was more than what separated them: the genuine desire to do what was best for West Indies cricket. In that context my facilitation of a resolution was made much easier. Further, the West Indies people were tired of this festering pimple; the conflict had gone on for far too long; the people rightly concluded that it was much ado about nothing and demanded its prompt resolution. The relative ease with which Gayle's re-entry into the Test team has been effected confirms a long-established practice in human endeavours that one is not required to be a dinner pal of someone else to work productively with him or her in any collective enterprise.

Often persons in authority who are entrusted with the responsibility to guide and manage modern, young men, tend to forget that the remarkable thing about them is that they are young people living in changing, modern times with altering cultural practices, different but not necessarily worse than before. Gayle and Ramnaresh Sarwan are in their early 30s; Jerome Taylor has just gone past his mid-20s. Authoritative leadership is required to understand them and help to mould them on paths which are conducive to success and nobility in life and cricket. We must not only instill in them a bundle of virtues but more importantly we must draw out of them that which is good, noble and worthy in them; and there is an abundance of goodness, nobility and worth in these young men and others. It is my view that discipline, narrowly conceived, cannot be taught; one teaches and guides a whole human being, who in the process grasps that discipline, self-restraint, and an orderly, productive life delivering optimal results from him/her, for himself/herself and our civilisation.

Equally, the young men on the cricket team, or in any field of endeavour, must recognise the responsibilities which go with their blessings of skills, health, strength and intelligence. Self-development in solidarity with the collective – the team, the community, the nation, the region — is vital. The individual *qua* individual has to give way to the concept and reality of the social individual who has an organic connection with the community and nation which have brought the person thus far. The apotheosis of the atomized individual, made manifest in the later years of Howard Hughes' life, rich and surrounded by lots of people none of whom he can truly trust, is a species of loneliness, sadness, and pathos unbecoming of a civilised human condition.

From my private discussions with Gayle, I am satisfied that he fully understands the necessity and desirability of a strong nexus between the individual and his community and nation so as to avoid, on the one hand, a crass and naked individualism, and on the other, an unreal denial of self. I am satisfied, too, from my telephone conversations with Sarwan that he has grasped all this. After all, they have come from good families, God-fearing communities, have experienced the solidarity with collectives (cricket teams, family, community, nation and region), and have abundant blessings for which they are thankful and humbled. Authority structures must appreciate that every human being has different, not necessarily worse, personality traits, and who must always be respected. Always, there must be mutual respect; authority ought however to exercise greater magnanimity, mindful that the greatest exercise of authority is the restraint in the use of that authority. That was Worrell's way! This was the approach which he urged, unsuccessfully, upon the WICB on the occasion of its conflicts with the rural proletarian Jamaican, the tearaway fast-bowler Roy Gilchrist in the period 1958 to 1960.

It is evident to every reasonable, objective observer that the WICB and its subordinate affiliates or entities require reform in their structures of governance and the lifting of their performances. A useful starting point is P. J. Patterson's report on the governance of West Indies cricket. Cricket administrators appear to the public to be too self-serving, aloof, inattentive to detail, less-than respectful to players who question authority, and insufficiently accountable to their constituents and the West Indian people on whose behalf they are entrusted responsibility for the development and protection of a public good, West Indian cricket. But, overwhelmingly, the men and women who run West Indies cricket are individual human beings of merit, worth and goodness. I will not be party to the unseemly "ad hominem" attacks on worthy men and women by those who hanker to replace them without any or any compelling narrative of meaningful change for the better.

Too often in the Caribbean mirages are conjured up through demagogic critiques and an absence of a coherent, developmental vision, philosophy, policy, and implementable programme of action. There are no quick-fixes to our challenges in cricket, society, and political economy. A relatively impecunious WICB, when compared to the Boards in India, England, Australia, New Zealand, and South Africa, cannot work magic in countries which are themselves reeling from the impact of the global economic meltdown and natural disasters. Further, the WICB and West Indies cricket are being more severely buffeted and undermined, objectively-speaking, by IPL than any other major test-cricketing nation. The challenge here is not so much an insufficiency of patriotism and nationalism, but an inadequacy of financial resources to compete with an encroaching cricket imperialism of India's turbo-charged capitalism and the dictates of a massive market. A similar process is at work in the poaching of talented footballers from Latin America and Africa to lucrative club football in Europe. The big difference is that a football match lasts ninety minutes and a test cricket game needs five days; a cricket test series between two countries requires two-to-three months; and there are several of these per year for the eight test-cricketing nations. Thus, a footballer from Brazil playing for Manchester United or

Barcelona is granted a release from his European club to play the match or a few matches over a few days for his nation, in accordance with the regulations of the international football authority, FIFA. The nature of the game of cricket and the international cricket schedule are not easy to be reconciled with an insurgency like IPL. But a workable solution must be found to satisfy, as far as humanly practicable, the various stakeholders.

I have been informed by the President of the WICB, Julian Hunte, that his Board has elaborated a Strategic Plan for the development of West Indies Cricket. This is to be discussed shortly with CARICOM's Prime Ministerial Sub-Committee on Cricket. Before this plan is finalised it ought to be put in the public domain for extensive consultation. Once a coherent plan is in place to be implemented through reformed governance structures, the issue of appropriate personnel to lead the WICB then comes to the fore with urgency. But changing the faces at the top of WICB is a futility without a "compelling narrative", without a properly-fashioned Strategic Plan and detailed Work Programme, and without reformed governance arrangements. Rebuilding West Indies cricket is serious business for serious people which will take a long time. But we must start now and have the people fully engaged.

Often I hear shrill voices from some governments and the mass media of communication that West Indian governments must become centrally involved in the management of West Indies cricket because the game touches so many people and because the governments have invested hundreds of millions of dollars in top quality cricket facilities. I have no time for such voices or arguments; they are entirely fallacious.

First of all, West Indian governments run so many things badly. Why would they ever want to get into the management of West Indies cricket? They build roads and bridges for even more millions of dollars, should they run mini-buses, taxis, and all road transport? They construct expensive seaports, so the governments must run ships which ply our region? If West Indian governments ever get into the management of cricket, nationally or regionally, they would mash it up. Look at what is happening in Pakistan. In any event the ICC would rightly not countenance undue political interference in our cricket.

Clearly though, a reasonable case can be made for a partnership between governments and the WICB, structured in such a way that does not infringe upon the Board's independence of action. At the same time this "independence" cannot be conceived as a separateness which, in practice, amounts to a suicide pact. After all, any Strategic Plan for Cricket would require the support of the governments, the private sector and other non-State actors if it is to be successfully implemented. These entities and prominent individuals ought to be structured into an appropriate Consultative Mechanism to meet on an agreed basis with the WICB to discuss all relevant aspects of regional cricket. But purely cricketing decisions are the province of the WICB, not the governments. In any event the Consultative Mechanism cannot be a decision-making body; the WICB is the decision-making authority.

I hear, too, some unfortunate, critical noises from some responsible quarters in the region, especially out of Guyana, Jamaica, and Trinidad and Tobago about the management of West Indies cricket, which flow from petty territorial nationalism or even chauvinism. Some even talk about "going it alone" in test cricket, an anathema to Frank Worrell who always sought to strengthen cricket's regionalism, and obviously unsustainable in the modern cricket world. I hear unseemly public quarrels about the distribution of test matches and one-day internationals across the ten countries which now have test cricket facilities. It is evident that some countries would be left out for one, two or even three years, depending on the number of international matches to be played. Worst of all, deplorable prattle comes to my ears that it is unacceptable for the President and Chief Executive Officer of WICB, and the captain of the West Indies to hail from one country, St. Lucia. This kind of internecine madness must stop! We ought to celebrate the fact, as Worrell no doubt would have done, that leading administrators and test cricketers now come from all West Indian territories, including those from and beyond the traditional "big Four" of Barbados, Guyana, Jamaica and Trinidad and Tobago. Indeed, Worrell plugged actively in his day for greater participation of players and administrators from the Windward and Leeward Islands. He was a leader ahead of his times.

I make bold to say that despite the profound limitations of the WICB as currently structured and constituted, it is much more democratic, more open and transparent, more sensitive to players' concerns, and more responsive to the public than the Boards of yesteryear manned by representatives of the planter-merchant elite. Still there is much more to be done by the current WICB to win the confidence of the general public, the players, the "legends" of the past, and the governments; it simply must lift its game. To combat the more deleterious effects to our cricket of the virtually unstoppable cricket juggernaut which is the BCCI and IPL and the jostling elements for administrative dominance from England and Australia, the West Indies cricket team must return to its halcyon days of cricket supremacy. This must be coupled with a creative, developmental, and assertive WICB, in the interest of our people at home and in the diaspora, including a treasured space for our women and their cricket. Quality West Indies cricket, quality ideas, quality administrative systems, quality management, and a sufficiency of material resources for the game at home, would again put our cricket on top of the world.

The cultural and sociological barriers, which constitute the main encumbrances to our cricket's renaissance, have to be tackled not only for cricket but for living and production. Imitativeness, especially the worst features of American and European society, must be eschewed. Laziness, which is an absence of virtue, must be curbed; growing ill-discipline and lawlessness are to be rooted out; coarseness in public discourse must be avoided; and "learned helplessness" must be isolated and defeated. A rebirth in our cricket is possible if we embrace, conceptually and practically, a thorough-going sense of self-mastery in our Caribbean civilisation in our seascape and landscape in which we are not merely transient travelers but owners of our own destiny and our patrimony.

Worrell's Humanism and Final Memorial

Worrell's humanism is our light, a brightness which illuminates and does not blind; that very human love and caring which propelled him to come to Nari Contractor's aid with life-saving blood on February 03, 1962, a day celebrated each year in the Indian state of West Bengal as "Sir Frank Worrell Day", is our continuing inspiration and motivation.

We look to our future with hope knowing that there are burdens to carry, many rivers to cross, many crosses to bear, but also conscious of our strengths and possibilities which will renew us. To be sure, our faith will see us through, a faith made perfect, made complete by works. That is our challenge. It is our redemption song!

In a closing memorial to Frank Worrell, I summon the aid of C. L. R. James in his essay "Cricket in West Indian Culture" published in *New Society*, 6 June, 1963:

> When (in 1961) over a quarter of a million people in an Australian city came into the streets to tell Worrell's team goodbye, a spontaneous gesture of affection and respect, the West Indies, clearing their way with bat and ball, had made a public entry into the comity of nations. It has been done under the aegis of the men who more than all others created the British public-school tradition, Thomas Arnold, Thomas Hughes, and W.G. Grace. They would recognise Frank Worrell as a representative of all they were and stood for. But juniors grow up and have to make their own independent way. In cricket, the West Indies have evolved a style of their own, even if in independence as a whole they have yet to do so.

So, from yesterday we come with our burdens; tomorrow we go forth confidently with our strengths!

Made in the USA
Middletown, DE
02 February 2016